EDMONDS

BEGINNER'S
COOKBOOK

Hodder Moa

Tableware kindly supplied by **Milly's Kitchen of Ponsonby** and **Living & Giving**

National Library of New Zealand Cataloguing-in-Publication Data
Lyons, Sue.
Edmonds beginner's cookbook / [recipes developed by Sue Lyons ;
photography by Bruce Benson ; illustrations by Deborah Hinde].
Includes index.
ISBN-13: 978-1-86971-075-0
ISBN-10: 1-86971-075-4
1.Cookery. I. Benson, Bruce. II. Hinde, Deborah, 1957- III. Title.
641.512—dc 22

A Hodder Moa Book
Published in 2006 by Hachette Livre NZ Ltd
4 Whetu Place, Mairangi Bay
Auckland, New Zealand

Reprinted 2007, 2009 (twice)

Text, illustrations and photographs © Goodman Fielder New Zealand Limited 2006
Design and format © Hachette Livre NZ Ltd 2006

All rights reserved. No part of this publication may be reproduced or transmitted in any form or by any means, electronic or mechanical, including photocopying, recording, or any information storage and retrieval system, without permission in writing from the publisher.

Designed and produced by Hachette Livre NZ Ltd
Text and food styling by Sue Lyons
Photographs by Bruce Benson
Illustrations by Deborah Hinde
Printed by Toppan Printing Co, China

Front cover: Decorated Chocolate Brownie Muffin, page 102

CONTENTS

How To . . .	4
1. Breakfasts, Snacks and Soups	9
2. Main Meals and Salads	33
3. Desserts	81
4. Baking	97
Menu Ideas	132
Index	134

HOW TO...

COOK PERFECT RICE

The absorption method is an easy way to produce perfect rice. Wash rice thoroughly before cooking to remove excess starch by placing in a sieve and rinsing under cold running water until the water runs clear. Place rice in a heavy-based saucepan. Add enough cold water to cover rice by 2 cm. Cover pan with a tight-fitting lid. Bring to the boil over a high heat, then reduce heat to very low. Cover and cook for about 15 minutes or until all the liquid is absorbed. Remove from heat and stand, covered, for 5 minutes. Use a fork to fluff up the rice.

CRUSH GARLIC (WITHOUT A GARLIC CRUSHER)

Place garlic clove on a chopping board. Put the flat blade of a cook's knife on the clove and press hard with your hand. Peel off skin. Chop garlic roughly. Place a little salt on the chopping board, then top with chopped garlic. Using the flat blade of a cook's knife, squash garlic into salt with a backward and forward motion.

DUST WITH ICING SUGAR

Spoon a little icing sugar into a fine sieve. Hold over the food to be dusted then shake gently so icing sugar passes through the sieve and falls onto the surface of the food.

FOLD

The method used to combine a light mixture with a heavy one. With a metal spoon, use a cutting action to cut down through the centre, bringing the bottom mixture to the top.

GRATE PARMESAN CHEESE

Use a fine grater to grate this cheese, for use in pasta dishes, pesto and on top of pizzas. It is best not to use pre-grated parmesan, as the flavour is not quite as good as freshly grated.

GRILL BACON

Preheat oven grill. Lay bacon rashers in a single layer in a metal baking dish. Grill until bacon begins to crisp.

KNEAD

To press non-yeast doughs (such as biscuit dough) together to get an even texture. Yeast doughs (such as pizza dough) are stretched and folded so they become elastic. This is done by pushing the dough away from you with the heel of your hand, then folding the dough over.

MAKE COOKED RICE INTO A MOULDED SHAPE

Grease the inside of a teacup or small bowl. Spoon in the hot rice and press firmly. Turn the bowl upside down onto the serving plate. Holding the plate and bowl, shake with a couple of firm movements. Remove the bowl. (See photograph on page 59.)

MAKE PORK AND BEEF EASIER TO SLICE

Cover and place in the freezer for 20 minutes (before cooking).

MELT CHOCOLATE

Care is needed when melting chocolate. Intense heat will cause the chocolate to turn into an unusable lump. To melt on the **stove top**, place water to a level of 3 cm in a small saucepan. Bring to the boil. Sit a tight-fitting heatproof bowl over saucepan, ensuring the bowl does not touch the water. Add chocolate and stir constantly over just simmering water until chocolate has melted. To melt in a **microwave** oven, place chocolate in a microwave-proof bowl. Microwave on 50% power for 30 seconds. Stir. Repeat this process until chocolate has melted.

SERVE ICE-CREAM IN PERFECT BALLS

Use an ice-cream scoop to serve ice-cream or semifreddo. Dip the scoop in a glass of lukewarm water, then dry the scoop — this stops the ice-cream from sticking to it.

SHRED CHICKEN

Remove skin and bones from chicken. Tear into strips.

SIFT

To pass dry ingredients (such as flour or cocoa) through fine mesh to remove lumps or to mix evenly.

SIMMER

To cook just at boiling point, not a full rolling boil.

STIR-FRY

To stir and toss prepared ingredients in hot oil very quickly, resulting in moist meats and crisp vegetables.

TOAST/ROAST NUTS

Place nuts in an ovenproof dish and cook at 180°C for 5–15 minutes, depending on the nuts, until light golden. Toss during cooking.

TOAST COCONUT AND SEEDS

Place coconut or sunflower seeds or sesame seeds in a frying pan. Cook over a medium heat, stirring frequently, until light golden.

USE BAKING PAPER

This has a special coating on it to prevent food sticking. It saves greasing baking tins or trays.

USE FISH SAUCE

This is one of the most important ingredients in Thai cooking. It is made from salted fish (usually anchovies) which are fermented, so use only a little. Don't be put off by the strong smell, this disappears with cooking.

This symbol means '**an idea**'. We give you ideas for extra things that you might like to do to make the recipe even better.

This symbols means '**a cooking tip**'. We give you tips to make sure that the recipe is successful.

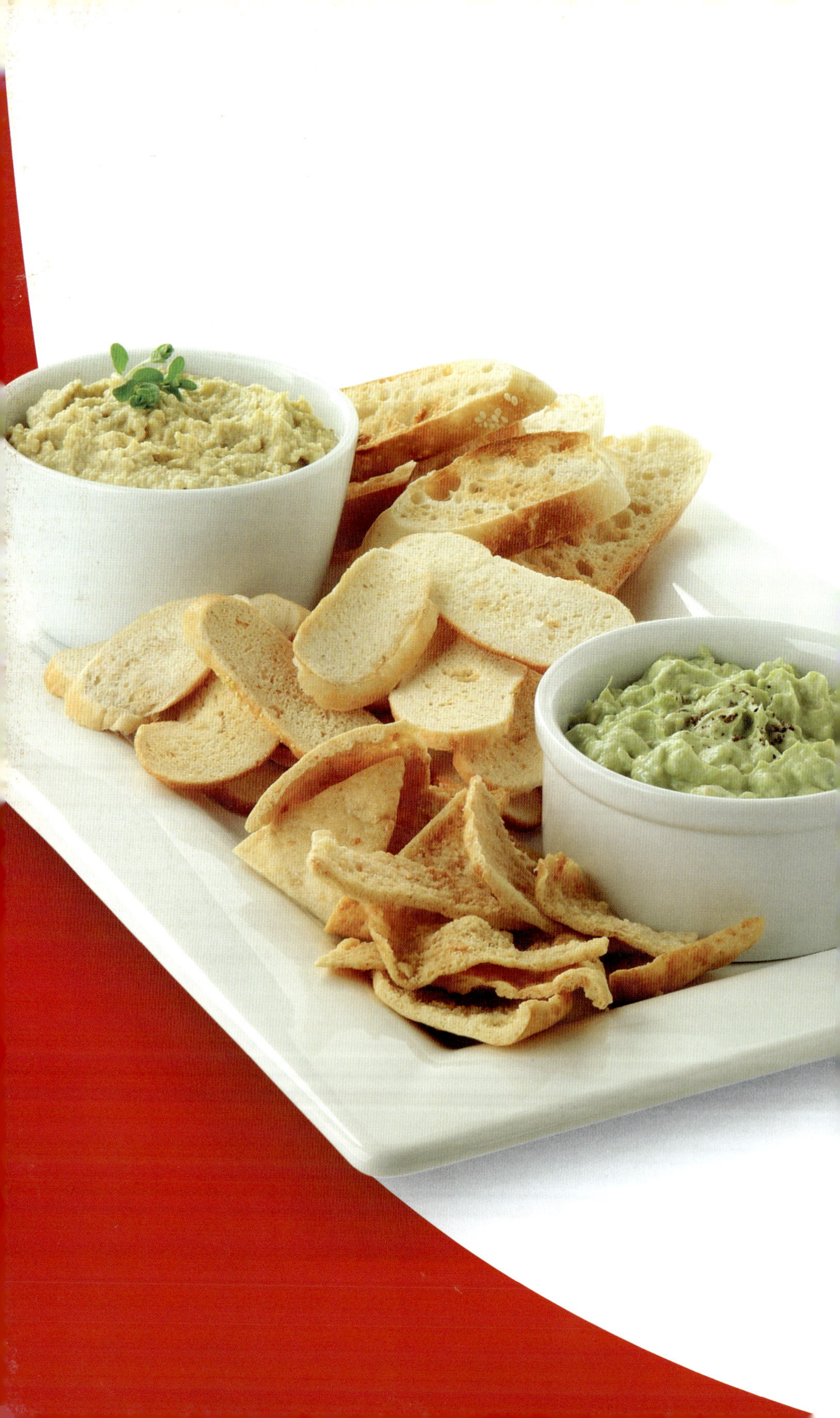

BREAKFASTS, SNACKS AND SOUPS

Try these recipes for a **great** start to the day or a **yummy** easy-to-make 'in between' meal.

Top left: Hummus (page 18)
Bottom right: Guacamole (page 19)

TOASTED MUESLI

Makes 7 cups

The whole family will love this crunchy muesli. Serve with diced fresh fruit and yoghurt for a healthy start to the day.

- 3 cups wholegrain rolled oats
- 1 cup thread coconut
- ½ cup wheatgerm
- ½ cup nuts or seeds, e.g. sunflower seeds, pumpkin kernels, hazelnuts or chopped Brazil nuts
- 1 teaspoon cinnamon
- ⅓ cup Amco canola oil
- ⅓ cup liquid honey
- 1 cup raisins or sultanas
- ¾ cup chopped dried apricots

1 Preheat the oven to 190°C. Combine the oats, coconut, wheatgerm, nuts and cinnamon in a roasting dish. Mix well.

2 Drizzle over the oil and honey. Mix well.

3 Bake for 25–30 minutes or until golden, stirring every 5 minutes.

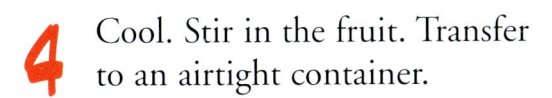

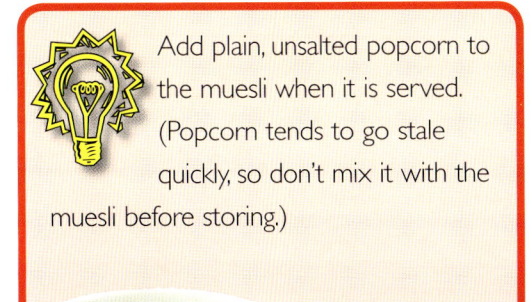

4 Cool. Stir in the fruit. Transfer to an airtight container.

Add plain, unsalted popcorn to the muesli when it is served. (Popcorn tends to go stale quickly, so don't mix it with the muesli before storing.)

PANCAKES

Makes about 6–8 pancakes

Pancakes are a favourite weekend breakfast treat. Serve them with sliced banana and cinnamon sugar for a real café-style breakfast!

1 cup Champion standard grade flour
⅛ teaspoon salt
1 egg
about 1 cup milk
butter to grease

To serve
sliced banana
Greek yoghurt
lemon wedges
1 tablespoon caster sugar
pinch of cinnamon

1 Sift the flour and salt into a bowl. Add the egg and mix lightly with a fork.

2 Gradually add the milk, mixing constantly with a wooden spoon, until smooth.

3 Cover with plastic food wrap and refrigerate for 1 hour — the batter will thicken.

4 Grease a small frying pan with butter. Heat the pan. Pour in enough batter to just cover the base of the pan.

5 Cook for about 2 minutes until golden on the bottom.

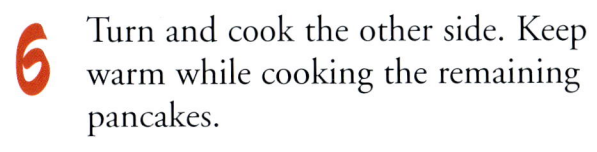

6 Turn and cook the other side. Keep warm while cooking the remaining pancakes.

7 To serve, fold pancakes into quarters. Arrange 2 pancakes on each serving plate. Arrange sliced bananas on the side. Place a spoonful of yoghurt and a lemon wedge next to the pancakes. Combine sugar and cinnamon, then sprinkle over pancakes and yoghurt.

FRENCH TOAST

Set yourself up for the day, or enjoy French Toast for brunch after a weekend sleep in!

2 eggs
2 tablespoons milk
salt and freshly ground black pepper to season
4 slices toast-cut bread (wholemeal or white)
butter to grease
maple syrup and/or grilled Kiwi bacon to serve, optional
sprigs of mint to garnish, optional

1 Place the eggs and milk in a bowl. Beat until they are combined. Season with a little salt and pepper.

2 Cut each slice of bread in half diagonally, so that you have 2 triangles.

3 Melt a little butter in a frying pan over low to medium heat.

4 Dip the bread triangles in the egg and milk mixture, one at a time. Place in the frying pan and cook for about 2 minutes until golden on the bottom.

5 Turn and cook for a further 2 minutes until golden. Serve with a drizzle of maple syrup and grilled bacon, if you like. Garnish with a sprig of mint.

THE COOLEST DRINKS

Makes 2 x 300 ml smoothies

You will need a blender or food processor to make these delicious drinks.

Slushies

Use your favourite fruit juice for these super-refreshing drinks. Freshly squeezed juices are best — don't use juice with added sugar or preservatives. Freeze several containers of juice so you can make slushies whenever you want.

1 Pour the juice (allowing 300 ml per drink) into a shallow plastic or glass container to a depth of 1.5–2 cm. Cover and freeze until frozen.

2 Remove the frozen juice from the freezer and stand for 10 minutes. Turn out onto a chopping board and cut into pieces.

3 Place the frozen juice in a blender or food processor. Pulse until slushy.

4 Transfer to a serving glass. Pour a little fruit juice over the ice so that the mixture is slushy. If you like, place a slice of lime or lemon over the edge of the glass.

Fruit and Yoghurt Smoothie

For a low-fat smoothie, use non-fat milk and reduced-fat yoghurt. Make a Fruit and Yoghurt Super Smoothie by adding 1 scoop of vanilla ice-cream or frozen yoghurt to the blender.

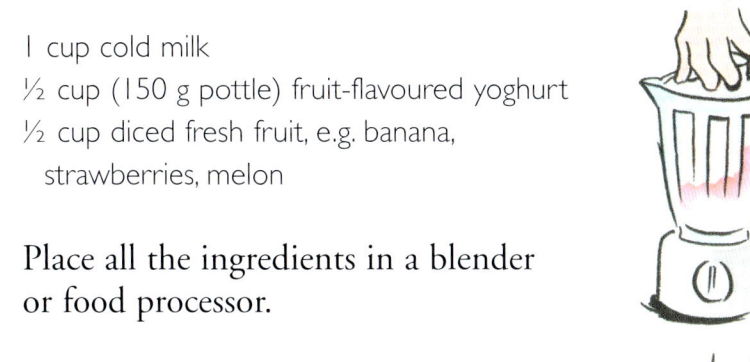

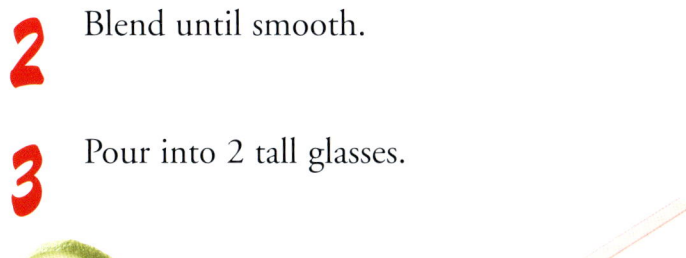

1 cup cold milk
½ cup (150 g pottle) fruit-flavoured yoghurt
½ cup diced fresh fruit, e.g. banana, strawberries, melon

1 Place all the ingredients in a blender or food processor.

2 Blend until smooth.

3 Pour into 2 tall glasses.

HUMMUS

Makes 2 cups

Placed in a small pottle, hummus is a great lunchbox addition. Include a plastic knife for spreading it onto toasted Turkish bread, pita bread or crackers. (See photograph on page 8.)

2 x 300 g cans chickpeas (or 2 cups cooked chickpeas)
1 onion, finely sliced
1 clove garlic, roughly chopped
2 tablespoons tahini (see Cook's Tip)
1 teaspoon ground cumin
¼ cup olive oil
2 tablespoons lemon juice
salt and freshly ground black pepper to season
sprig of fresh herbs to garnish, optional

1 Tip the chickpeas into a sieve and rinse them under cold running water. Drain thoroughly.

2 Place all the ingredients in a food processor. Blend until smooth.

3 Place the hummus in a serving bowl. Cover and refrigerate until needed. Garnish with a sprig of fresh herbs.

- Tahini is a Middle Eastern paste made from sesame seeds. You will find it in most supermarkets.
- Covered and refrigerated, hummus will keep for up to 2 weeks.

GUACAMOLE

Makes about ¾ cup

Guacamole can be prepared several hours before you need it and stored in the refrigerator. To stop the guacamole discolouring, place the avocado stone back into the prepared Guacamole and place plastic food wrap directly over the surface of the Guacamole. (See photograph on page 8.)

1 ripe avocado
¼ cup sour cream
2 teaspoons lemon juice
few drops Tabasco Sauce
salt and freshly ground black pepper to season

1 Cut the avocado in half. Remove the stone. Scoop out the flesh and place in a bowl.

2 Using a fork, mash the flesh lightly.

3 Mix in the sour cream, lemon juice and Tabasco. Season with a little salt and pepper.

4 Place the guacamole in a serving bowl. Sprinkle over a little cracked pepper to garnish. Serve immediately.

PESTO

Pesto is a wonderful Italian invention! A thick paste-like sauce, pesto is traditionally made with fresh basil, garlic, pine nuts, parmesan cheese, olive oil and salt and pepper.

Basil Pesto
(makes ½ cup)

1 cup basil leaves, lightly packed
⅓ cup freshly grated parmesan cheese
⅓ cup toasted pine nuts (page 7)
⅓ cup extra virgin olive oil
2 cloves garlic, roughly chopped
salt and freshly ground black pepper to season

Walnut and Parsley Pesto
(makes ¾ cup)

1 cup Italian (flat-leaf) parsley leaves, lightly packed
½ cup good-quality walnuts, toasted (page 7)
¼ cup freshly grated parmesan cheese
¼ cup extra virgin olive oil
salt and freshly ground black pepper to season

To make both these pestos, place all the ingredients in a food processor. Blend to a thick paste. Transfer to a small container. Cover and store in the refrigerator. Pesto will keep for about 2 weeks.

- Use extra virgin olive oil for pesto (and dressings), as it is the best-quality olive oil and will give the best flavour.
- Good-quality walnuts are important — the oil in walnuts has a tendency to go rancid or stale. Look for walnuts that are plump and golden in colour. To keep all nuts fresh, store them in the freezer.
- Pesto can be frozen — place in ice-cube trays, freeze, then transfer to a resealable plastic bag and return to the freezer.

BRUSCHETTA

Some wonderful Italian breads do go stale quickly, but in Italy every last crumb is used. Bruschetta is one way the Italians use leftover or stale bread. Use a chewy ciabatta or other European-style bread which are available from some supermarkets or specialty bread shops. Traditionally, bruschetta are made by grilling the bread over a wood fire, then drizzling it with olive oil. Sometimes the grilled bread is then rubbed with a cut clove of garlic.

8 slices ciabatta or other European-style bread, cut into 1 cm-thick slices
olive oil to brush

1 Preheat the oven to 190°C. Using a pastry brush, brush both sides of each slice of bread with olive oil. Place on a baking tray.

2 Bake for 12–15 minutes, turning over once during this time. Remove from the oven. Cool. Store in an airtight container until needed.

Topping Suggestions
Arrange toppings on bruschetta, then serve immediately.

Basil Pesto and Tomato — spread cooked bruschetta with Basil Pesto (page 20).

Arrange sliced vine-ripened tomatoes on top. Drizzle over a little extra virgin olive oil. Garnish with tiny basil leaves. Season lightly with salt and freshly ground black pepper.

Walnut Pesto, Pear and Parmesan — spread cooked bruschetta with Walnut and Parsley Pesto (page 20). Using a vegetable peeler, shave parmesan from a block. Arrange on pesto. Top with finely sliced pear. Drizzle over a little extra virgin olive oil. Season lightly with salt and freshly ground black pepper.

CHICKEN WRAPS

Wraps are a great alternative to regular sandwiches. The filling combos are endless — here is one idea to get you started on a Wrap addiction!

flatbread (try Quality Bakers Wraps)
Guacamole (page 19) or
  Hummus (page 18), optional
lettuce leaves, washed and dried
cooked shredded chicken (see Cook's Tip)
salad ingredients of your choice,
  e.g. sliced tomato and avocado,
  mung bean sprouts or Tabbouleh
  (page 38)
mayonnaise to spread

1 Lay the flatbread on a flat surface. Spread lightly with Guacamole or Hummus.

2 Arrange the lettuce in a line down one long edge of the flatbread.

3 Top with the chicken and salad ingredients or Tabbouleh. Spread with a little mayonnaise.

4 Roll the flatbread up around the filling to form a log. Trim off the ends, then cut in half diagonally. Wrap a serviette or a piece of folded baking paper around the middle of each half, tucking in the ends.

Leftover roast chicken is perfect for shredding. The rotisserie chickens, available at most supermarkets, are great too.

CHEESE AND SALSA QUESADILLAS

Quesadillas are a Mexican-style toasted sandwich. They are delicious served with Guacamole (page 19).

    2 cups cooked shredded chicken (see Cook's Tip page 25)
    1½ cups grated tasty cheddar cheese
    ½ cup bottled tomato salsa
    8 × 20-cm-diameter flour tortillas

1 Combine the chicken, cheese and salsa in a bowl.

2 Lay 4 of the tortillas on a flat surface. Spread with the chicken mixture to within 1 cm of the edge.

3 Sandwich with the remaining tortillas and press down lightly with a flat hand.

4 Heat a large frying pan. Using a fish slice, place 1 tortilla 'sandwich' in the pan.

5 Cook over a medium heat for 2 minutes. Carefully turn over and cook for another 2 minutes.

6 Remove from the pan. Repeat with the remaining tortillas. To serve, cut into wedges. Serve with Guacamole, if you like.

Pumpkin Soup

Serves 2–3

Warm up on the coldest of winter's days with this healthy Pumpkin Soup. This recipe can be doubled, to serve 4–6 people. It freezes well.

- 2 cups chopped, peeled pumpkin
- 1 medium potato, peeled and chopped
- 1 carrot, peeled and chopped
- 1 onion, chopped
- 2½ cups water
- 1 teaspoon brown sugar
- ½ teaspoon curry powder
- ⅛ teaspoon cinnamon
- salt and freshly ground black pepper to season
- fresh crusty bread to serve

1 Combine all the ingredients except the salt and pepper in a medium saucepan.

2 Cover the pan and bring to the boil. Reduce the heat and simmer for 25 minutes, until the vegetables are soft. Take the pan off the heat. Set it aside to cool for 20 minutes.

3 Transfer half of the soup to a food processor. Blend until smooth. Transfer to a bowl.

4 Blend the rest of the soup until smooth in food processor.

5 Tip all the soup back into the saucepan. Heat gently. Season with salt and pepper.

6 Ladle into warm bowls or mugs. Serve with fresh crusty bread.

CORN AND CHICKEN SOUP

Serves 2–3

You can make this soup as a light meal then follow it with one of the delicious desserts from page 81 onwards.

1 boneless, skinless chicken breast
25 g butter
2 tablespoons Champion standard grade flour
3 cups chicken stock
300 g can cream-style corn
salt and freshly ground black pepper to season
Italian (flat-leaf) parsley leaves to garnish
fresh crusty bread to serve

1 Cut the chicken into tiny pieces. Set it aside.

2 Melt the butter in a medium-sized saucepan. Add the flour and stir constantly for 1 minute.

3 Take the pan off the heat. Gradually add the stock, stirring constantly.

4 Return the pan to the heat, stirring constantly until the sauce boils.

5 Add the chicken and corn. Stir for 3–4 minutes, until the chicken is cooked and the soup is hot. Season with salt and pepper.

6 Ladle into warm bowls. Garnish with Italian parsley and ground black pepper. Serve with fresh crusty bread.

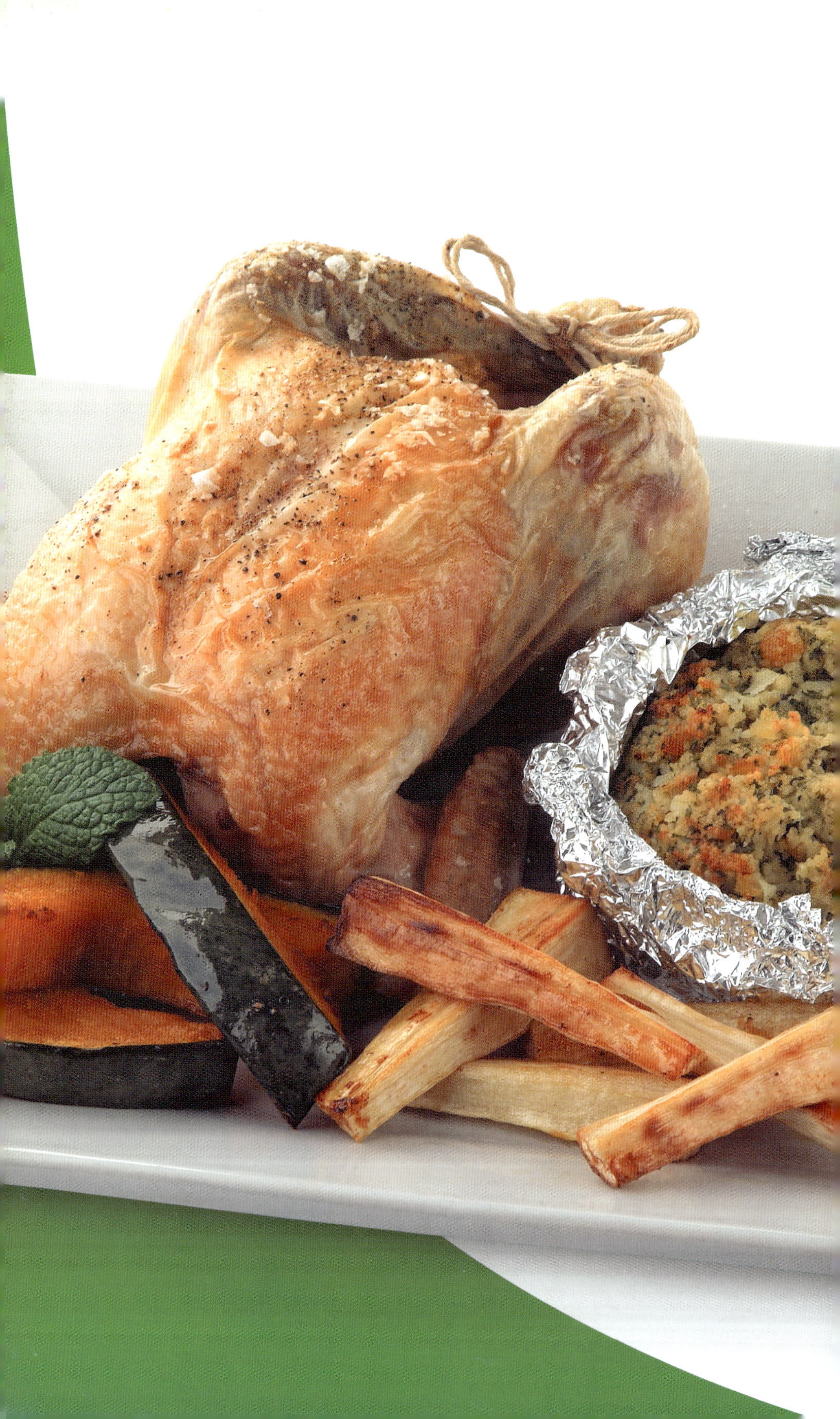

MAIN MEALS AND SALADS

Your friends and family will **love** these **delicious** meals. Check out page 132 for more ideas on how to use these recipes.

Roast Chicken with Moroccan Couscous Stuffing (page 78)

CAESAR SALAD

Serves 4

Serve Caesar Salad for lunch or as a light dinner meal. If you prefer chicken to bacon, try the Chicken Caesar Salad. Did you know that Caesar Salad has nothing to do with Julius Caesar? It was invented by chef Caesar Cardini.

Croutons
4 thick slices white bread (toast cut or any white bread cut into thick slices)
2 tablespoons olive oil

Salad
6 slices Kiwi bacon
2 teaspoons olive oil
1 cos lettuce, washed
shavings of parmesan cheese (see Cook's Tip)
¼ cup prepared Caesar dressing (available from supermarkets)

1 To make the croutons, cut the bread into cubes about 2 cm square. Heat the oil in a frying pan. Add the bread cubes. Toss often, until golden. Remove from the pan and set aside.

2 Cut the rind off the bacon (this is not needed). Chop the bacon into bite-size pieces. Heat the oil in a frying pan. Cook the bacon, stirring often, until it begins to crisp. Remove from the pan and set aside.

3 If the lettuce leaves are large, tear them into pieces. Place the lettuce in a serving bowl. Add the bacon and parmesan. Toss lightly.

4 Divide the salad between 4 serving plates. Scatter over the croutons.

5 Drizzle the dressing over salads. (If the dressing is very thick, it can be thinned slightly by stirring through a little lemon juice before adding to the salad.) Serve the salad immediately.

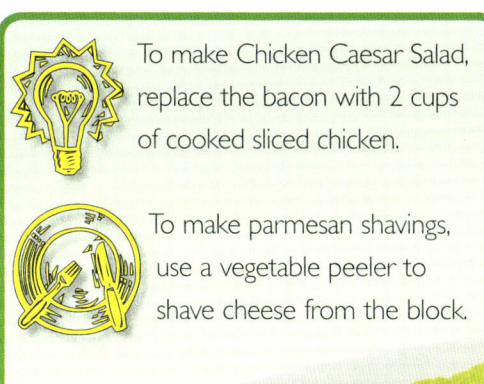

To make Chicken Caesar Salad, replace the bacon with 2 cups of cooked sliced chicken.

To make parmesan shavings, use a vegetable peeler to shave cheese from the block.

TUNA SALAD

Serves 4 as a lunch or light meal

This delicious, healthy salad can be served in lots of different ways: on a bed of shredded lettuce, in pita pockets or as a wrap, rolled in flatbread.

20 cm-length telegraph cucumber
3 tomatoes or 20 cherry tomatoes
2 x 185 g cans tuna in water, drained
½ avocado, sliced
¼ cup mayonnaise
2 teaspoons lemon juice
a little salt and freshly ground black pepper to season
½ iceberg lettuce, washed and finely shredded (sliced)
fresh bread, to serve

1 Cut the cucumber in half lengthwise, then cut each piece in half again, lengthwise. Slice into 5 mm-thick pieces.

2 Cut the tomatoes in half, then cut each half into 4 wedges. If using cherry tomatoes, cut in half.

3 Place the cucumber and tomatoes in a bowl. Using a fork, gently flake the tuna into the bowl. Add the avocado.

4 Toss very lightly to combine. Combine the mayonnaise and lemon juice. Season with salt and pepper.

5 Divide the shredded lettuce between 4 serving plates. Spoon the salad on top. Drizzle the dressing over the salad ingredients. Serve with crusty bread.

Serving Suggestions

Tear pita bread in half. Stuff with shredded lettuce and Tuna Salad. Or make a Tuna Wrap, following the Chicken Wrap instructions on page 24, but replace chicken with Tuna Salad.

Add any of these ingredients to the salad: cooked French beans, pitted olives, hard-boiled eggs that have been shelled and quartered, capers. For a more substantial salad, add cooked, cooled pasta or cooked, cooled diced potatoes.

TABBOULEH

This Middle Eastern salad is a great side dish. It is often served as an entrée in Lebanese meals.

1 cup bulgur (cracked wheat)
2 tablespoons chopped fresh mint
1 cup chopped parsley
2 spring onions, finely sliced
2 tomatoes, chopped
2 tablespoons olive oil
¼ cup lemon juice
salt and freshly ground black pepper

1 Put the bulgur in a bowl. Cover with boiling water. Leave it to stand for 30 minutes.

2 Stir the bulgur and drain off any remaining water.

3 Combine all the ingredients in a bowl. Mix well.

Serving Suggestions

Serve with Falafel (page 42). You could also include it in a Chicken Wrap (page 24).

Bulgur is available from the bulk bins of most supermarkets. It is also called 'burghul' and 'cracked wheat'.

OMELETTE

If the cupboards are almost bare, you can always whip up an omelette!

2 eggs
1 tablespoon milk
salt and freshly ground black pepper
butter to grease
sprig of parsley to garnish

1 In a bowl, lightly beat together the egg and milk. Add a little salt and pepper.

2 Heat a 20-cm omelette pan or frying pan. Add a small knob of butter and tilt the pan around so the butter melts evenly over the base.

3 Pour in the egg mixture. Cook over a medium heat, lifting the edges of the omelette with a spatula, so the uncooked egg runs underneath. Continue cooking until the egg is set and golden.

4 Loosen from the pan with a spatula, then fold in half.

5 Place on a serving plate. Garnish with parsley.

> When the omelette is set and golden, scatter grated tasty cheddar cheese over one half. Loosen from the pan with a spatula and fold the plain half over the cheese. The warmth of the omelette will melt the cheese slightly — yum!

FALAFEL IN PITA BREAD WITH GARLIC SAUCE

Makes 36 falafels

Another Middle Eastern treat. Be a really clever cook and make your own Hummus (page 18) and Tabbouleh (page 38) to serve with this Falafel.

2 x 300 g cans chickpeas in brine, drained
1 stalk celery, chopped
1 teaspoon crushed garlic
2 tablespoons Champion standard grade flour
2 tablespoons tahini (sesame paste)
1 teaspoon ground cumin
½ teaspoon turmeric
½ teaspoon salt
freshly ground black pepper to season
Champion standard grade flour to coat
vegetable oil to cook
pita bread to serve
Hummus (page 18) and Tabbouleh (page 38) to serve

1 Place all the ingredients in a food processor except the flour to coat and oil. Blend until coarse.

2 Transfer to a bowl. Cover with plastic food wrap and refrigerate for 1 hour.

3 Spread a little flour onto a flat plate. Take large teaspoonsful of the mixture and roll into balls, then roll in flour to lightly coat. Flatten patties slightly with the palm of your hand.

4 Pour the oil into a frying pan to a level of 1 cm. Heat the pan over a medium heat. Cook the falafels for about 5 minutes or until golden, turning once.

5 Drain on paper towels. Use falafel and salad ingredients to fill pita bread. Drizzle some Garlic Sauce (see recipe below) over it, if you like.

Garlic Sauce
¾ cup natural unsweetened yoghurt
½ teaspoon crushed garlic
freshly ground black pepper to season

Combine all ingredients. Mix well.

HAM FRITTATA

A frittata is an Italian-style omelette. It can be served in many ways: hot with a fresh green salad or cold for a picnic or in a lunchbox. You can also serve Frittata in thin wedges as a starter.

2 tablespoons Amco canola oil
1 onion, finely chopped
1 cup small broccoli florets, optional
2 cloves garlic, crushed
1 tablespoon Dijon mustard
8 eggs
salt and freshly ground black pepper to season
2 cups diced cooked potatoes (about 2 large potatoes)
4 slices ham, diced
1½ cups grated tasty cheddar cheese

1 Heat the oil in a heavy-based frying pan with a heatproof handle. Cook onion, broccoli, garlic and mustard over a medium heat for 5 minutes.

2 Lightly beat the eggs with salt and pepper.

3 Add the potatoes and ham to the pan and stir. Spread evenly over the base of the pan. Turn the heat down to low. Pour the beaten eggs evenly over the vegetable and ham mixture. Sprinkle with cheese.

4 Cook for about 8 minutes until the frittata is half cooked. Meanwhile, preheat the oven grill.

5 Place the frittata under the grill for 3–4 minutes until set and golden. Leave in the pan for 5 minutes before cutting it into wedges. Serve warm or at room temperature with a green salad.

> Take care placing the pan under the grill — the pan, its handle and the grill will all be very hot!

STUFFED BAKED POTATOES

Nothing beats a good stuffed potato. If you are on a budget, Stuffed Baked Potatoes are an economical meal.

medium-large potatoes, washed and dried
oil to brush
a little butter and milk to mash
salt and freshly ground black pepper to season
grated tasty cheddar cheese to sprinkle

Suggested Fillings
diced cooked bacon, chopped spring onions and grated tasty cheddar cheese
flaked, drained tinned tuna or salmon, chopped parsley and grated tasty cheddar cheese
baked beans and grated tasty cheddar cheese
diced cooked bacon and diced avocado

1 Preheat the oven to 180°C. Prick the potatoes several times with a fork. Cut a slice off the bottom of each potato so that they sit flat. Use a paper towel to rub the potatoes all over with oil.

2 Place the potatoes directly onto the oven rack. Bake for 1–1¼ hours or until tender when pierced with a sharp knife. Stand for 5 minutes. Increase oven temperature to 220°C.

3 Slice the top off each potato. Hold each potato in a clean teatowel (as the potato will still be hot). Scoop the flesh into a bowl, leaving a 5 mm-thick shell.

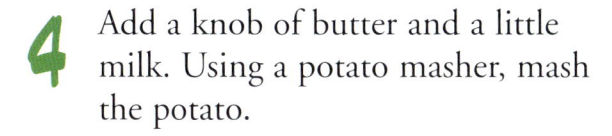

4 Add a knob of butter and a little milk. Using a potato masher, mash the potato.

5 Gently stir in the filling of your choice. Season with salt and pepper. Pile the mixture back into the shells. Sprinkle with grated cheese.

6 Place the potatoes on an oven tray. Bake for 15 minutes.

PASTA ALLA CARBONARA

Serves 4

Spaghetti alla Carbonara is one of the most popular pasta dishes. Its beginnings are not known for sure, but it is thought to have come from Rome. Spaghetti alla Carbonara means 'charcoal-makers spaghetti'. The dish could have got this name because the specks of pepper that season it look like ash from old-fashioned charcoal-making. The name may also have come about because Spaghetti alla Carbonara may have kept these Italian craftsmen well fed while they worked long, hard hours.

2 teaspoons olive oil
8 rashers rindless Kiwi bacon
400 g Diamond pasta shapes, e.g. penne
3 eggs
½ cup cream
½ cup freshly grated parmesan cheese
salt and freshly grated black pepper to season

1 Heat the oil in a heavy-based frying pan. Cook the bacon for 6–8 minutes until almost crisp and the pan is dry. Take off the heat.

2 Cook the pasta following the instructions on the packet.

3 While the pasta is cooking, whisk together the eggs, cream, parmesan and salt and pepper.

4 Drain the pasta thoroughly, then return to the saucepan. Toss through the egg mixture and bacon.

5 Return to a low heat and toss for 30 seconds to allow the eggs to cook. Do not overheat or the egg mixture will scramble.

6 Serve immediately.

PASTA WITH PESTO, BACON AND PEAS

This quick and easy pasta dish will be a hit with the entire family! Make it extra special by making the pesto yourself (page 20).

> 8 slices (400 g) shoulder or middle Kiwi bacon
> 400 g Diamond pasta shapes, e.g. penne or spirals
> 2 teaspoons olive oil
> 1½ cups frozen peas
> ⅓ cup pesto (any type of pesto can be used)
> a little salt and freshly ground black pepper to season
> shavings of parmesan cheese to serve (see Cook's Tip on page 35)

1 Remove any rind from the bacon, it is not needed. Chop the bacon into bite-size pieces.

2 Put a large saucepan of water on to boil. Add a pinch of salt.

3 Add the pasta and cook following the instructions on the packet, or until 'al dente' (firm when you bite it).

4 While the pasta is cooking, heat the oil in a frying pan. Cook the bacon for 6–8 minutes, stirring often, until the bacon just begins to crisp.

5 Just before the pasta is cooked, place the peas in a small microwave-proof bowl. Add 1 tablespoon of water. Cover and cook on high power for 2 minutes. Drain.

6 Drain the pasta in a sieve. Return to the saucepan and stir through the pesto. Add the bacon and peas. Toss to combine. Season with salt and pepper.

7 Serve immediately. Scatter over parmesan shavings, if you like.

- Cut 15 cherry tomatoes in half. Toss through the pasta with cooked bacon and peas.
- Toss ½ cup walnut pieces through the pasta with cooked bacon and peas.

MACARONI CHEESE

Serves 4

An old favourite, Macaroni Cheese can be baked in small, individual ovenproof dishes.

1½ cups Diamond macaroni elbows

White Sauce
50 g butter
1 small onion, finely chopped
¼ cup Champion standard grade flour
½ teaspoon dry mustard, optional
2 cups milk
1 cup grated tasty cheddar cheese
salt and freshly ground black pepper to season

Topping
1 cup grated tasty cheddar cheese

1 Cook macaroni following the instructions on the packet. Meanwhile, make the sauce.

2 For the sauce, place butter in a saucepan. Melt over a low heat. Add the onion and cook for 5 minutes until it is soft.

3 Add the flour and stir constantly for 2 minutes. Remove from heat. Stir in the mustard. Gradually add the milk, stirring constantly.

4 Return the pan to the heat, stirring constantly until the sauce is thick and comes to the boil.

5 Take off the heat. Stir in the cheese. Season with salt and pepper.

6 Preheat the oven to 180°C. Stir the macaroni into the cheese sauce. Place in an ovenproof dish. Sprinkle the cheese reserved for the topping over the macaroni. Bake for 20 minutes or until golden.

Add chopped ham to the macaroni mixture when stirring in the cheese.

PIZZA BASE

Serves 4

This quantity of dough will make two crispy-crust pizzas or one thick-crust pizza. When rolling out the dough you don't need to be too fussy about the circle being perfectly round!

1 tablespoon Edmonds active yeast
½ teaspoon sugar
300 ml warm water
1 teaspoon salt
3 cups Champion high grade flour
1 tablespoon olive oil

Note: As an alternative to making the pizza base, use a 30-cm-diameter commercial pizza base or 4 pita breads.

1 Mix the yeast, sugar and water together in a bowl. Leave in a warm place for 10 minutes until frothy.

2 Mix the salt and flour together in a large bowl. Add the yeast mixture and oil. Mix until ingredients form a soft dough. Sprinkle flour onto a clean, dry work surface. Knead the dough for 5 minutes until smooth and stretchy.

3 Lightly oil a large bowl. Sit the dough in the bowl and cover with a clean teatowel. Stand in a warm place until the dough doubles in size. This will take about 45 minutes.

4 Lightly grease an oven tray. Preheat the oven to 220°C.

5 Push your fist into the middle of the dough. Place on a lightly floured surface and knead for 1 minute.

6 Roll the dough into a 30-cm-diameter circle to make one thick-crust pizza. For thin-crust pizzas, divide the dough in half. Roll out each piece to a thickness of about 3 mm.

7 Cover the pizza base lightly, to within 1 cm of the edge of the dough, with prepared tomato sauce (you can buy pizza sauce at most supermarkets). Top with any of the combinations on page 56 or create your own toppings. Bake for 15 minutes until golden.

- A pizza wheel is a great tool to have — it makes cutting pizza a breeze.
- Pizza dough can be frozen after it has risen. Thaw it out at room temperature before using.

PIZZA TOPPINGS

Greek Pizza
Diced feta cheese, halved pitted olives, thinly sliced red onion, sliced sundried tomatoes or halved cherry tomatoes and grated mozzarella or tasty cheddar cheese. Garnish cooked pizza with oregano leaves or torn basil leaves.

Hawaiian Pizza
Diced ham, drained unsweetened pineapple pieces and grated mozzarella or tasty cheddar cheese.

Mushroom and Salami Pizza
Diced salami, sliced mushrooms, sliced red or green pepper and grated mozzarella or tasty cheddar cheese.

Chicken and Pesto
Thinly spread pizza base with pesto instead of tomato sauce. Sprinkle with a thin covering of grated mozzarella or tasty cheese. Top with shredded, cooked chicken, chopped spring onions and halved cherry tomatoes. Sprinkle over enough cheese to lightly cover the topping.

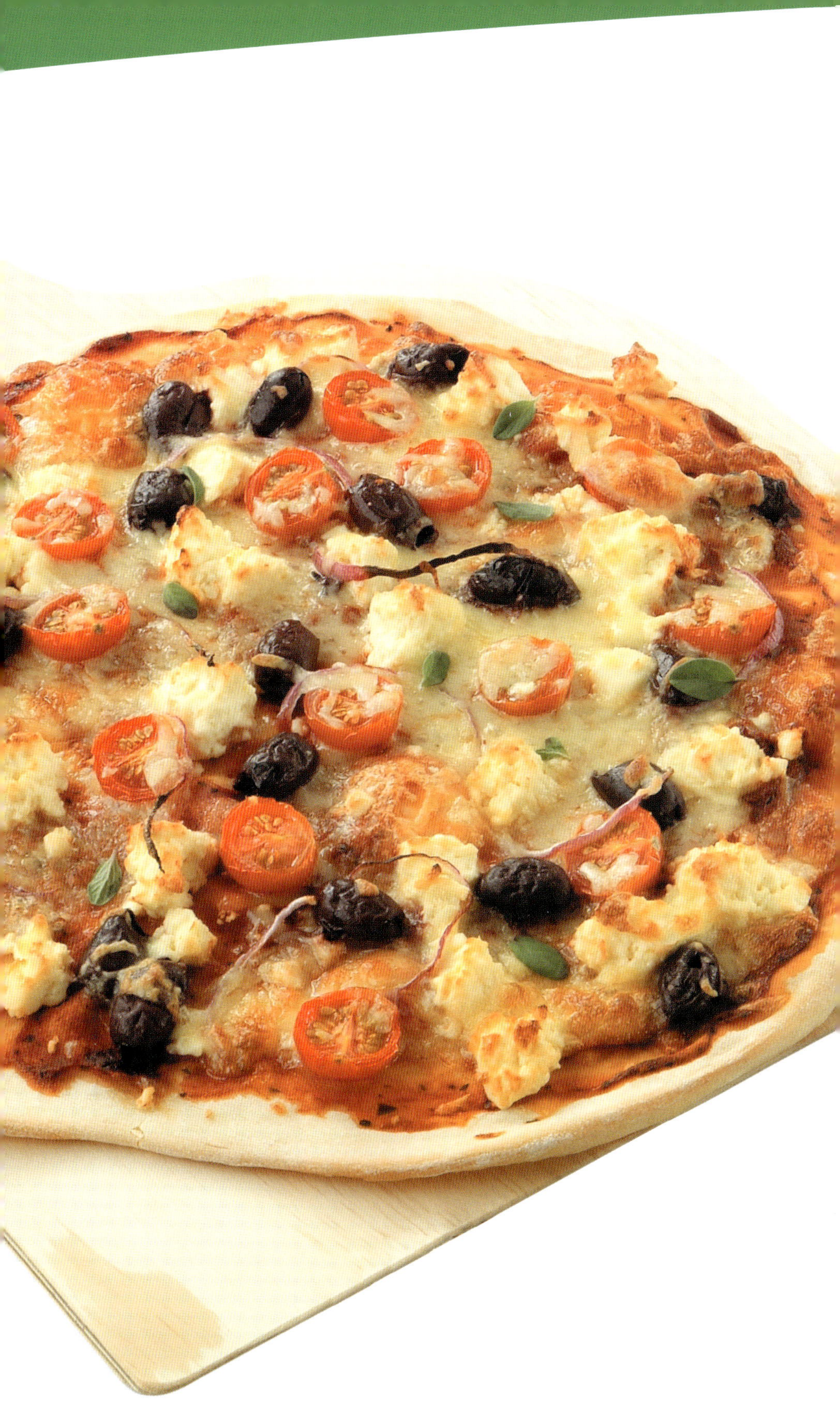

CHICKEN KEBABS
WITH QUICK PEANUT SAUCE

Serves 4

Vary the following recipe by including vegetables such as mushrooms and courgettes on the skewers.

12 wooden skewers (about 8 cm long)
4 boneless, skinless chicken breasts, or 600 g rump steak
¼ cup soy sauce
2 tablespoons honey
2 tablespoons lemon juice
1 tablespoon Amco canola oil
2 red peppers, cut into 1.5-cm cubes
24 chunks pineapple
cooked rice to serve (page 4)

1 Soak the skewers in cold water for 30 minutes — this stops the skewers burning when cooking.

2 Cut the chicken or steak into bite-size pieces (about 2-cm cubes).

3 Mix the soy sauce, honey, lemon juice and oil together in a bowl. Add the meat. Stir to coat. Cover and refrigerate for 1 hour.

4 Thread meat, pepper and pineapple onto the skewers.

5 Place in a single layer on a baking tray, if grilling in an oven.

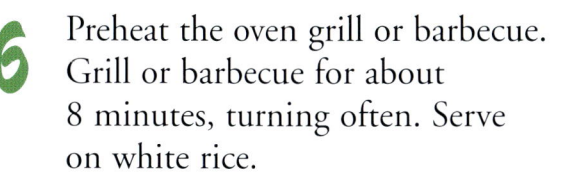

6 Preheat the oven grill or barbecue. Grill or barbecue for about 8 minutes, turning often. Serve on white rice.

Quick Peanut Sauce

1 teaspoon Amco canola oil
1 small onion, finely chopped
1 cup crunchy peanut butter
¾ cup coconut milk
1 tablespoon chilli sauce, optional

Heat the oil in a small saucepan. Cook the onion for 4–5 minutes until soft. Add the peanut butter, milk and chilli sauce (optional) to pan. Stir over a low heat for 3–4 minutes until smooth. Transfer to a serving bowl.

HAMBURGERS

Makes 6 hamburgers

Traditionally, hamburgers are made by sandwiching a cooked, round meat patty and salad ingredients between a toasted bun. With such a variety of specialty breads so widely available, you can create your own signature burgers — try squares of focaccia bread and shape the patties into squares to fit the bread.

500 g lean minced beef
1 small onion, finely chopped
2 cloves garlic, crushed
2 tablespoons tomato sauce
2 tablespoons Amco canola oil
6 hamburger buns
butter to spread
lettuce leaves
sliced cheese
sliced tomato
sliced beetroot, optional
sliced avocado, optional
tomato sauce, optional

1 Mix together the beef, onion, garlic and tomato sauce. Divide the mince mixture into 6 equal portions. Press each into a saucer to make a patty about 7 cm in diameter.

2 Heat the oil in a frying pan. Cook the patties for 6 minutes on each side.

3 Preheat the oven grill. Cut the buns in half horizontally.

4 Place the buns on the oven tray and grill until golden. Lightly butter.

5 Place lettuce leaves then a meat patty on the bottom half. Top with your choice of cheese, tomato, beetroot and avocado. Spoon over a little tomato sauce, if you like. Cover with the top half of the bun.

To make Mini Hamburgers, use a small round biscuit cutter to stamp rounds from a flattish loaf of bread (such as Turkish bread or foccacia). Shape the patties the same size as the biscuit cutter too.

NACHOS

Serves 5

For a Mexican-themed meal serve Nachos with Guacamole (page 19).

Meat Sauce
1 tablespoon Amco canola oil
1 onion, chopped
500 g lean beef mince
2 cloves garlic, crushed
400 g can tomatoes in juice
2 tablespoons tomato paste
½ cup water
salt and freshly ground black pepper to season

440 g can chilli beans
200 g corn chips
1½ cups grated tasty cheddar cheese
sour cream to serve

1. Heat the oil in a frying pan. Cook the onion for 5 minutes until it is soft. Add the mince and garlic and cook until the mince is browned, stirring often.

2. Add the tomatoes, tomato paste and water, breaking up the tomatoes with a wooden spoon. Cook over a low heat for 30–35 minutes until the sauce is thick. Season with salt and pepper.

3 Add the beans and stir gently for 1–2 minutes to heat through. Preheat the oven to 180°C.

4 Scatter the corn chips over the base of a large ovenproof dish or 5 individual dishes. Warm in the oven for 5 minutes.

5 Turn the oven on to grill. Spoon the mince mixture over the chips. Sprinkle with cheese.

6 Grill for 3–4 minutes until the cheese melts and bubbles. Serve with sour cream and Guacamole.

Spaghetti and Meatballs

Serves 4

A cheap and cheerful meal that everyone will enjoy.

500 g lean beef mince
2 tablespoons tomato sauce
1 small onion, finely chopped
1 clove garlic, crushed
1 teaspoon curry powder
½ cup fresh breadcrumbs
500 g packet Diamond spaghetti
420 g can pasta sauce
finely sliced basil leaves to garnish, optional

1 Preheat the oven to 200°C. Mix the mince, tomato sauce, onion, garlic, curry powder and breadcrumbs together in a bowl. Mix well.

2 Roll tablespoonsful of the mixture into balls. Place them in a greased baking dish.

3 Cook for 10–12 minutes until cooked through, turning the meatballs once.

4 While the meatballs are cooking, cook the spaghetti following the instructions on the packet.

5 Heat the pasta sauce until hot. To serve, add the hot meatballs to the hot sauce, tossing to coat. Spoon on top of spaghetti. Scatter over sliced basil.

LASAGNE

Serves 5–6

You will be popular with the whole family when you serve this old favourite! It will take about 45 minutes to prepare before baking, so allow plenty of time.

ingredients for Meat Sauce (page 62)
ingredients for White Sauce (page 52)
150 g Diamond wide lasagne
1 cup grated tasty cheddar cheese

1 Make the Meat Sauce following steps 1–2 of the Nachos recipe on page 62.

2 Make White Sauce following steps 2–5 of the Macaroni Cheese recipe on page 52, leaving out the onion.

3 Half fill a large saucepan with water. Bring to the boil. Add the lasagne and stir with a fork. Boil for 6–8 minutes or until 'al dente' (firm when you bite it).

4 Drain the lasagne in a sieve. Preheat the oven to 180°C. Grease an ovenproof dish.

5 Spread half the meat sauce over the base of the dish. Arrange half the pasta on top of the sauce, then half the white sauce.

6 Repeat the layers in Step 5 once more. Sprinkle with cheese. Bake for 25 minutes.

WIENER SCHNITZEL

Serves 4

This is a famous traditional Austrian dish — 'wiener' is German for Viennese.

400 g wiener schnitzel
1 egg
2 tablespoons milk
¾ cup dry breadcrumbs
oil for frying
lemon wedges to garnish, optional

1 Trim the fat off the schnitzel and cut it into serving-sized pieces.

2 Whisk the egg and milk in a dish. Put the breadcrumbs in another dish.

3 Dip each piece of schnitzel in the egg to coat. Drain off the excess. Press each piece in breadcrumbs until coated on both sides.

4 Put on a plate. Cover and refrigerate for 1 hour.

5 Pour enough oil into a frying pan to generously cover the base. Heat the oil. Cook the schnitzel for 3–4 minutes on each side.

6 Drain on paper towels. Serve with mashed potato (see below) and a green vegetable. Garnish with a wedge of lemon.

Mashed Potatoes
One-third fill a saucepan with water. Add a pinch of salt. Bring to the boil. Peel potatoes and cut into quarters. Carefully lower into the water. Cover and simmer for 15–20 minutes, or until the potatoes are tender when pierced with a sharp knife. Drain the water. Add a small knob of butter and a little milk. Using a potato masher, mash the potatoes, adding a little more milk if necessary, until smooth and creamy. Finally, use a fork to whip the potatoes. Serve immediately.

THAI-STYLE SWEET AND SOUR PORK STIR-FRY

Serves 3–4

This delicious Thai-style dish is a variation on the traditional Chinese 'sweet and sour'. Have all the ingredients ready before you start cooking.

400 g lean pork, e.g. rump or leg steaks
2 tablespoons Amco canola oil
1 onion, sliced
3 cloves garlic, crushed
1 red pepper, seeded and thinly sliced
2 courgettes, cut into sticks
2 tomatoes, each cut into 8 wedges
225 g can pineapple pieces in natural juice (or ¾ cup fresh pineapple pieces)
3 tablespoons fish sauce (see page 7)
1 tablespoon sugar
2 spring onions, sliced
cooked rice to serve (page 4)

1 Cut the pork into thin slices.

2 Heat the oil in a wok or heavy-based frying pan. Stir-fry the onion and garlic over a medium heat for 2–3 minutes.

3 Add the pork, increase heat to high and stir-fry for 3–4 minutes.

4 Add the pepper, courgettes, tomatoes and pineapple to the pan. Stir-fry for 2–3 minutes.

5 Stir in the fish sauce and sugar. Cook for 2–3 minutes.

6 Add the spring onions. Toss to combine. Serve with cooked rice.

CHICKEN WITH BEANS AND HOKKIEN NOODLES

Serves 4

Chinese Hokkien noodles are available from most supermarkets or from Asian food stores. This recipe is very quick — it only takes 5–6 minutes to cook. Have all the ingredients ready before you start to cook.

¼ cup soy sauce
¼ cup water
2 tablespoons oyster sauce
400 g Hokkien noodles
2 tablespoons sesame oil (or Amco canola oil)
4 single skinless, boneless chicken breasts, thinly sliced
3 cloves garlic, crushed
2 teaspoons chopped fresh root ginger
200 g green beans, ends trimmed
3 cups mung bean sprouts
3 spring onions, sliced
coriander leaves for garnish, optional

1 Combine the soy sauce, water and oyster sauce in a bowl. Set aside.

2 Place the noodles in a bowl. Cover with hot water (from the tap). Stir the noodles with a fork to separate and leave to soak for 2–3 minutes. Drain in a sieve.

3 Heat the oil in a wok or heavy-based frying pan. Add the chicken to the pan and stir-fry over a high heat for 2 minutes.

4 Reduce the heat to medium. Add the garlic, ginger and beans and stir-fry for another 2 minutes. Stir in the soy sauce mixture. Stir-fry for 1 minute.

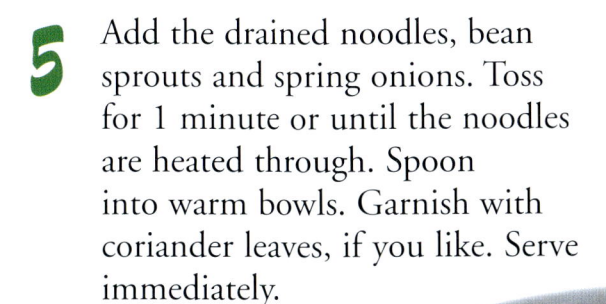

5 Add the drained noodles, bean sprouts and spring onions. Toss for 1 minute or until the noodles are heated through. Spoon into warm bowls. Garnish with coriander leaves, if you like. Serve immediately.

THAI-STYLE STIR-FRIED BEEF WITH PEANUTS

Serves 4

The small amount of Thai red curry paste used in this recipe does not make the dish too spicy, but does make a very tasty stir-fry!

750 g fast-fry beef steak, e.g. rump, porterhouse, fillet
2 tablespoons Amco canola oil
1 teaspoon crushed garlic
2 teaspoons Thai red curry paste
3 tablespoons fish sauce (page 7)
3 tablespoons oyster sauce
100 g green beans, ends trimmed
2 carrots, peeled and finely sliced
2 tablespoons chopped coriander
¾ cup roasted peanuts (page 7)
cooked rice to serve (page 4)

1 Trim the excess fat off the meat. Cut the meat into thin strips.

2 Heat the oil in a large heavy-based frying pan. Stir-fry the meat and garlic over a high heat for 3–4 minutes.

3 Add the curry paste, fish sauce, oyster sauce, beans and carrots. Stir-fry for 3–4 minutes.

4 Add the coriander and peanuts. Toss to combine.

5 Serve on a bed of cooked rice.

Slice the carrots finely so that they cook quickly.

SAUSAGES WITH MASH AND CHEESE

Serves 4

Try to use good-quality sausages for this recipe — ones that are not too fatty.

3 medium potatoes, peeled and quartered
8 sausages
a little Amco canola oil to cook
small knob of butter
about 2 tablespoons milk
¾ cup grated tasty cheddar cheese

1 Cook the potatoes in boiling water for about 20 minutes or until tender.

2 While the potatoes are cooking, prick the sausages once or twice with the point of a sharp knife. Cook the sausages in a frying pan with a little oil, or barbecue or grill in the oven.

3 Drain the potatoes. Add the butter and milk and mash using a potato masher.

4 Handling the hot, cooked sausages carefully, make a 1 cm-deep slit the length of each sausage.

5 Pile the mashed potato into the slits. Place the sausages side by side, potato-side up, in a shallow baking dish.

6 Sprinkle with cheese. Preheat the oven grill. Grill for 2–3 minutes until cheese melts and bubbles.

ROAST CHICKEN
WITH MOROCCAN COUSCOUS STUFFING

Serves 4

This easy and interesting stuffing is perfect for chicken. Couscous is a North African dish; the grains are made from semolina. (See photograph on page 32.)

Stuffing

1 tablespoon olive oil
1 small onion, finely chopped
¼ cup freshly squeezed orange juice (1 orange)
½ cup water
½ cup couscous
1 tablespoon butter
1 egg
⅓ cup finely chopped dried apricots
2 tablespoons chopped mint
2 tablespoons chopped coriander
salt and freshly ground black pepper to season

1.5 kg–1.7 kg whole chicken

1 Heat the oil in a small frying pan. Cook the onion for 5 minutes until it is soft. Remove from the heat.

2 Place the orange juice and water in a saucepan. Bring to the boil. Stir in the couscous. Remove the pan from the heat. Cover and stand for 2–3 minutes until the liquid has been absorbed.

3 Add the butter. Stir constantly over a very low heat for 2 minutes, using a fork to separate the grains.

4 Stir in the cooked onion, egg, apricots and herbs. Season with salt and pepper.

5 Preheat the oven to 180°C. Rinse the chicken inside and out under cold running water. Drain and pat dry with paper towels. Spoon the stuffing inside the chicken, pressing firmly with the back of a spoon.

6 Tie the legs together with string. Tuck the wing tips under the chicken. Place in a roasting dish, with the breast facing upwards. Brush the chicken with a little olive oil and season with salt and pepper. Bake, allowing 55 minutes per kilogram + 20 minutes extra (2 hours and 10 minutes for 1.5 kg chicken). Stand for 5–10 minutes before carving. Serve with roast vegetables.

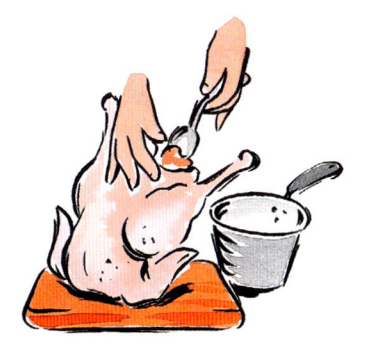

To cook chicken stuffing separately, lay a sheet of foil on a flat surface. Place the stuffing in a pile in the centre of the foil. Wrap the foil around the stuffing so that none can fall out. 45 minutes before the chicken is cooked, place the stuffing parcel directly on an oven rack. To serve, slice the stuffing using a sharp knife.

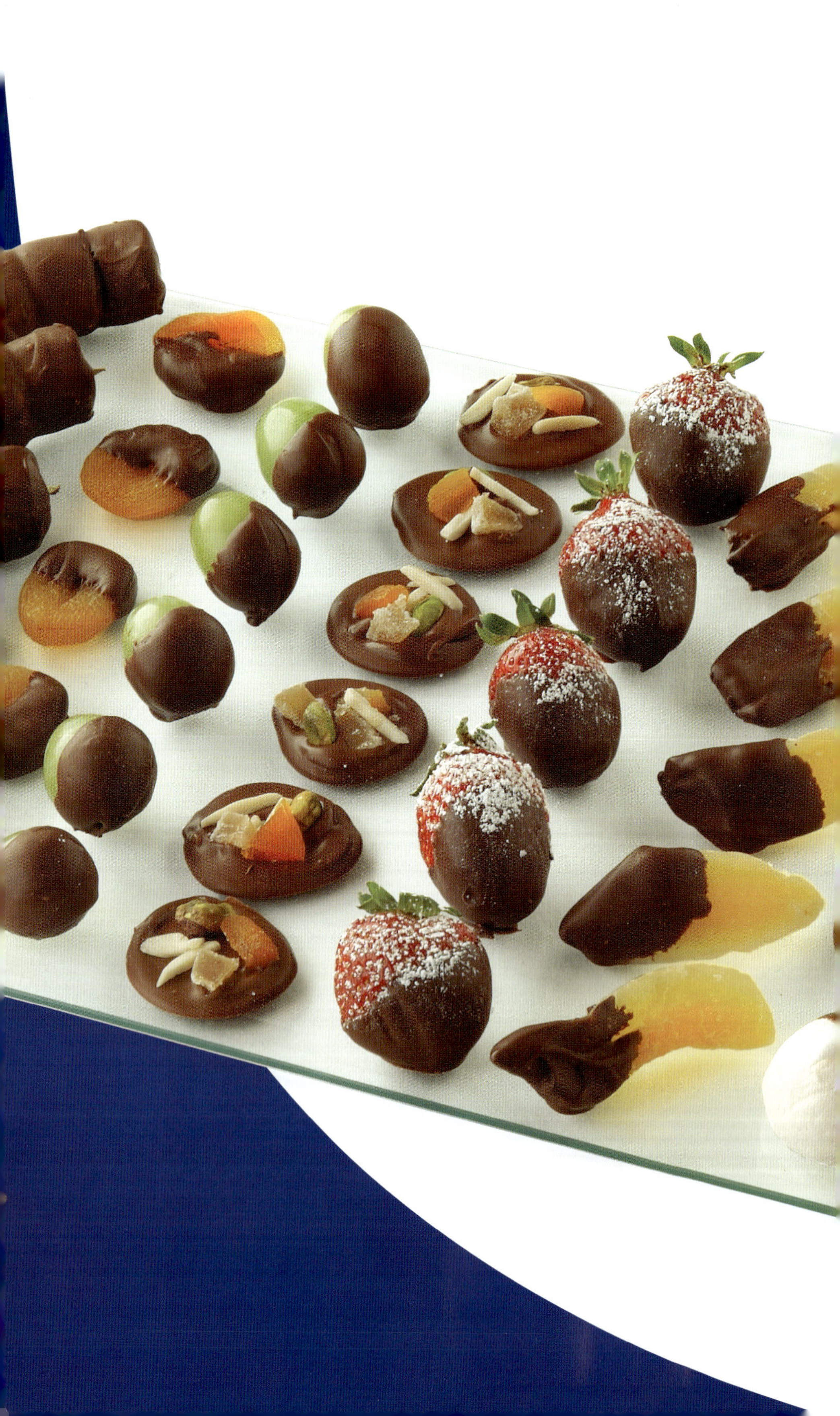

DESSERTS

A meal is not complete without a **mouth-watering** dessert! Everyone will **enjoy** these sweet treats.

Chocolate-dipped Treats (pages 84 and 85)

FRUIT SALAD

For a refreshing, healthy dessert you can't beat fruit salad. With a dollop of marshmallow yoghurt cream or passionfruit crème fraîche an old favourite can be made quite special.

Fruit Salad

Choose a selection of fresh fruit that is in season. During the summer months select from stone fruits such as apricots, nectarines and peaches, and berries such as strawberries and raspberries. Watermelon and other melons are a great addition. Over winter, when there is a more limited selection of fresh fruit available, use drained unsweetened canned fruit such as peaches, pears or apricots as a base for fruit salads. Add kiwifruit, oranges and banana. (Banana should be added just before serving as it goes brown quickly.)

To Prepare Fruit

Peel if necessary then slice or dice into bite-size pieces. Place in a serving bowl and toss gently.

Marshmallow Yoghurt Cream

¾ cup cream, whipped
150 g pottle (½ cup) fruit-flavoured yoghurt
12 marshmallows, halved

Gently fold together all the ingredients. Cover and refrigerate for at least 1 hour before serving to allow the marshmallows to soften.

Passionfruit Crème Fraîche

250 g pottle crème fraîche
¼ cup passionfruit pulp (about 3 passionfruit or use bottled passionfruit pulp)
1 tablespoon icing sugar

Gently fold together all the ingredients. Cover and refrigerate until needed.

CHOCOLATE-DIPPED TREATS

Makes 24 pieces

Use either dark, milk or white chocolate melts for these treats. If you want to create a wonderful platter of treats to serve a crowd, make the recipe twice, once using dark or milk chocolate, once using white chocolate. (See photograph on page 80.)

> ½ cup chocolate melts (dark, milk or white chocolate)
> 24 items for dipping, e.g. strawberries, grapes, dried apricots, dried rockmelon, giant marshmallows

1 Cover a plate or small tray with foil.

2 Melt the chocolate following the instructions on the packet, or as described on page 6.

3 Dip the items, one at a time, into the melted chocolate so that they are half covered. Place on the foil to dry. Strawberries should be served on the same day. Other items will keep for up to 1 week if stored in an airtight container in a cool place (not refrigerated).

Jewelled Chocolate Discs

½ cup chocolate melts (dark, milk or white chocolate)
1 tablespoon slivered almonds
14 pistachio nuts
2 or 3 dried apricots, cut into small pieces
3 pieces crystallised ginger, cut into small pieces

Cover a plate or small tray with baking paper. Melt the chocolate following the instructions on the packet, or as described on page 6. Working quickly, drop heaped teaspoonsful of chocolate on the baking paper, then spread to form a 4-cm disc. Quickly press one pistachio nut, one piece of ginger and apricot and several slivered almonds into each disc. Leave in a cool place to set. Store in an airtight container in a cool place (not in the refrigerator).

Makes 14

Chocolate Almond and Apricot Clusters

½ cup chocolate melts (dark, milk or white chocolate)
¼ cup slivered almonds
¼ cup finely chopped apricots

Cover a tray or flat plate with foil. Melt white or dark chocolate according to the instructions above. Stir slivered almonds and apricots into the melted chocolate. Drop tablespoonsful onto the foil. Set aside in a cool place to harden. Remove from the foil and store in an airtight container in a cool place (not in the refrigerator).

Makes 10–12

FUDGE PUDDING

Serves 4

Fudge Pudding is a great winter dessert. It is ideal to serve after a light meal, such as soup.

1 cup Champion standard grade flour
1 teaspoon Edmonds baking powder
2 tablespoons cocoa
¾ cup sugar
50 g butter
½ cup milk
1 teaspoon vanilla essence

Topping
½ cup brown sugar
1 tablespoon cocoa
1 cup hot instant coffee

cream to serve

1. Preheat the oven to 180°C. Grease a 5-cup-capacity ovenproof dish.

2. Sift the flour, baking powder and cocoa into a bowl. Stir in the sugar.

3. Place the butter and milk in a small saucepan. Stir over a low heat until the butter melts. Remove from the heat. Stir in the vanilla essence. Add the butter mixture to the dry ingredients. Mix well.

4 Spread the mixture evenly over the base of the dish.

5 To make the topping, mix the sugar and cocoa together in a cup. Sprinkle over the pudding. Carefully pour the coffee over the pudding — do not stir.

6 Bake for 40–45 minutes. Serve warm with cream.

LITTLE APPLE PIES

Makes 9 pies

These lovely apple pies are easy to make. Serve them warm with cream or ice-cream — or they are just as good served cold, as a snack.

2 pre-rolled sheets Irvines sweet shortcrust pastry (about 500 g)
380 g can diced apple
2 tablespoons caster sugar
¼ teaspoon cinnamon
icing sugar to dust
whipped cream or ice-cream to serve

1 Thaw the pastry following the instructions on the packet — about 15 minutes should be enough. Use as soon as it is thawed. Preheat the oven to 180°C.

2 Using a 7-cm round biscuit cutter, stamp 9 circles from each sheet of pastry. Line 9 deep muffin tins with a pastry circle.

3 Fill each pastry case with the diced apple. Combine the sugar and cinnamon. Sprinkle a little over each pie.

4 Using a pastry brush, brush the rim of each pie with a little water. Place remaining pastry circles over pies.

5 Use a fork and gently press around the edge of the pastry. Use the point of a knife to cut a small cross on the top of each pie — this allows the steam to escape. Refrigerate pies in muffin tins for 10 minutes.

6 Bake for 20–25 minutes, until golden. Stand in tins for 5 minutes before removing.

7 To serve, dust with icing sugar. Serve with whipped cream or ice-cream. Stored in the refrigerator these pies will keep for 2 days.

> Instead of covering the pies with a circle of pastry, try grating pastry and sprinkling over pies. To grate pastry, gather leftover pastry into a ball. Refrigerate for 10 minutes before grating coarsely.

MERINGUE NESTS

Serves 6

These Meringue Nests, like mini pavlovas, make an impressive dessert. Stored in an airtight container, they will keep for several days.

4 egg whites, at room temperature
1½ cups caster sugar
1 tablespoon Edmonds Fielder's cornflour
1 teaspoon DYC white vinegar
1 teaspoon vanilla essence
whipped cream
seasonal fresh fruit and/or grated chocolate

1 Draw six 10-cm circles on a sheet of baking paper large enough to cover a baking tray. Place paper on the baking tray. Preheat the oven to 180°C.

2 Using an electric mixer, beat egg whites until white and soft peaks form. Gradually add the sugar, beating constantly. Continue beating until thick and glossy.

3 In a small bowl, mix together the cornflour, vinegar and essence. Add to the egg white mixture. Beat on high speed for 5 more minutes.

4 Divide the mixture evenly between circles, spreading it to just within the edge of the circles, keeping the shapes as round as possible. Using the back of a spoon, make a slight hollow in the centre, to form a nest.

5 Place the tray in the oven, then turn down to 100°C. Bake for 50 minutes. Turn off the oven. Open the oven door slightly and leave the Meringue Nests until they are cold.

6 Carefully lift the nests onto individual plates. Decorate with whipped cream and fresh fruit and/or grated chocolate.

SEMIFREDDO

Makes about 2 litres

Semifreddo is Italian for 'half frozen'. It is similar to ice-cream, but softer, and is simpler to make. It does not require an ice-cream churn, but you will need an electric beater as the creamy texture is achieved by lots of beating! This should be eaten within 4 days of being made, as the eggs are not cooked.

Basic Recipe
4 eggs, separated
½ cup caster sugar
1 teaspoon vanilla essence
300 ml cream, whipped

1 Using an electric beater, beat the egg yolks and half of the caster sugar (¼ cup) until thick and pale. Beat in the essence.

2 In another bowl, beat the egg whites with an electric beater until soft peaks form. Gradually add the remaining sugar, 1 tablespoon at a time, beating well between each addition.

3 Using a metal spoon, gently fold the cream and flavourings of your choice (see page 93 for ideas) into the yolk mixture. Gently fold in the egg whites.

4 Transfer the mixture to a 2-litre glass, plastic or metal container. Cover and freeze for 4–5 hours or until firm.

Flavouring Suggestions

Raspberry — place 100 g raspberries (⅔ of a punnet) on a flat plate. Using a potato masher, squash raspberries to a pulp. Frozen raspberries can also be used. Thaw for 5–10 minutes before squashing.

Marshmallow and Coconut — toast ½ cup thread coconut (page 7). Using clean scissors, cut 25 marshmallows in half.

Marshmallow and Chocolate — using clean scissors, cut 20 marshmallows in half. Add ½ cup (100 g) chocolate chips or chopped chocolate.

Passionfruit — add ½ cup passionfruit pulp (about 7 passionfruit). Bottled passionfruit pulp can also be used.

ICE-CREAM SAUCES

Caramel Sauce

75 g butter
½ cup brown sugar
2 teaspoons Edmonds Fielder's cornflour
¼ cup cold water
¼ cup cream
ice-cream to serve

1 Put the butter and brown sugar in a small saucepan. Stir over a low heat until the mixture comes to the boil.

2 Simmer gently for 2 minutes. Remove from the heat.

3 Whisk the cornflour and cold water together in a cup. Slowly add it to the pan, stirring constantly.

4 Return the pan to the heat. Stir constantly until the sauce thickens and comes to the boil. Remove from the heat. Stir in the cream.

5 Serve over ice-cream.

Makes about 1 cup

Chocolate Sauce

2 tablespoons cocoa
1 teaspoon Edmonds Fielder's cornflour
25 g butter
¼ cup golden syrup
3 tablespoons water

1 Place all the ingredients in a microwave-proof jug. Stir well, until smooth. Cover with a paper towel.

2 Cook on Medium for 1 minute. Stir well.

3 Cook on Medium for a further 1½ minutes. Stand for 1 minute. Stir well.

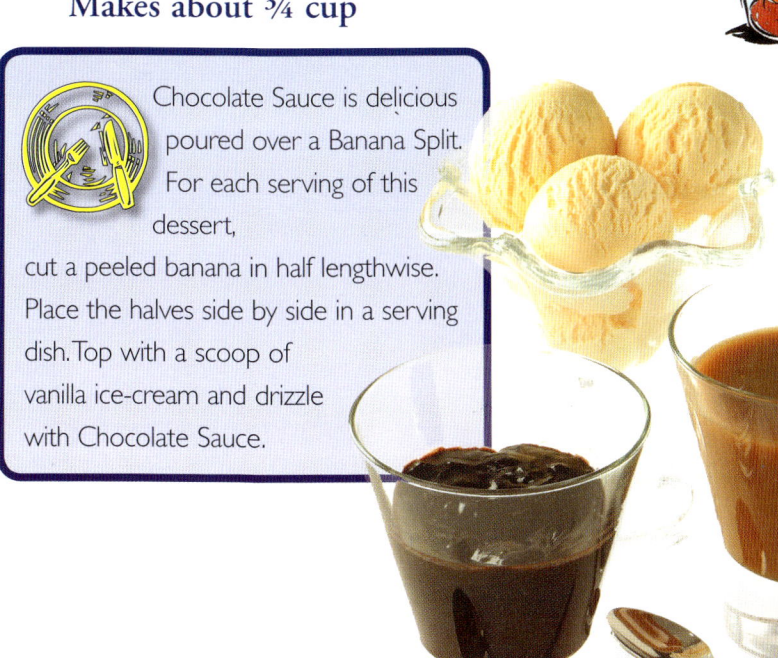

Makes about ¾ cup

Chocolate Sauce is delicious poured over a Banana Split. For each serving of this dessert, cut a peeled banana in half lengthwise. Place the halves side by side in a serving dish. Top with a scoop of vanilla ice-cream and drizzle with Chocolate Sauce.

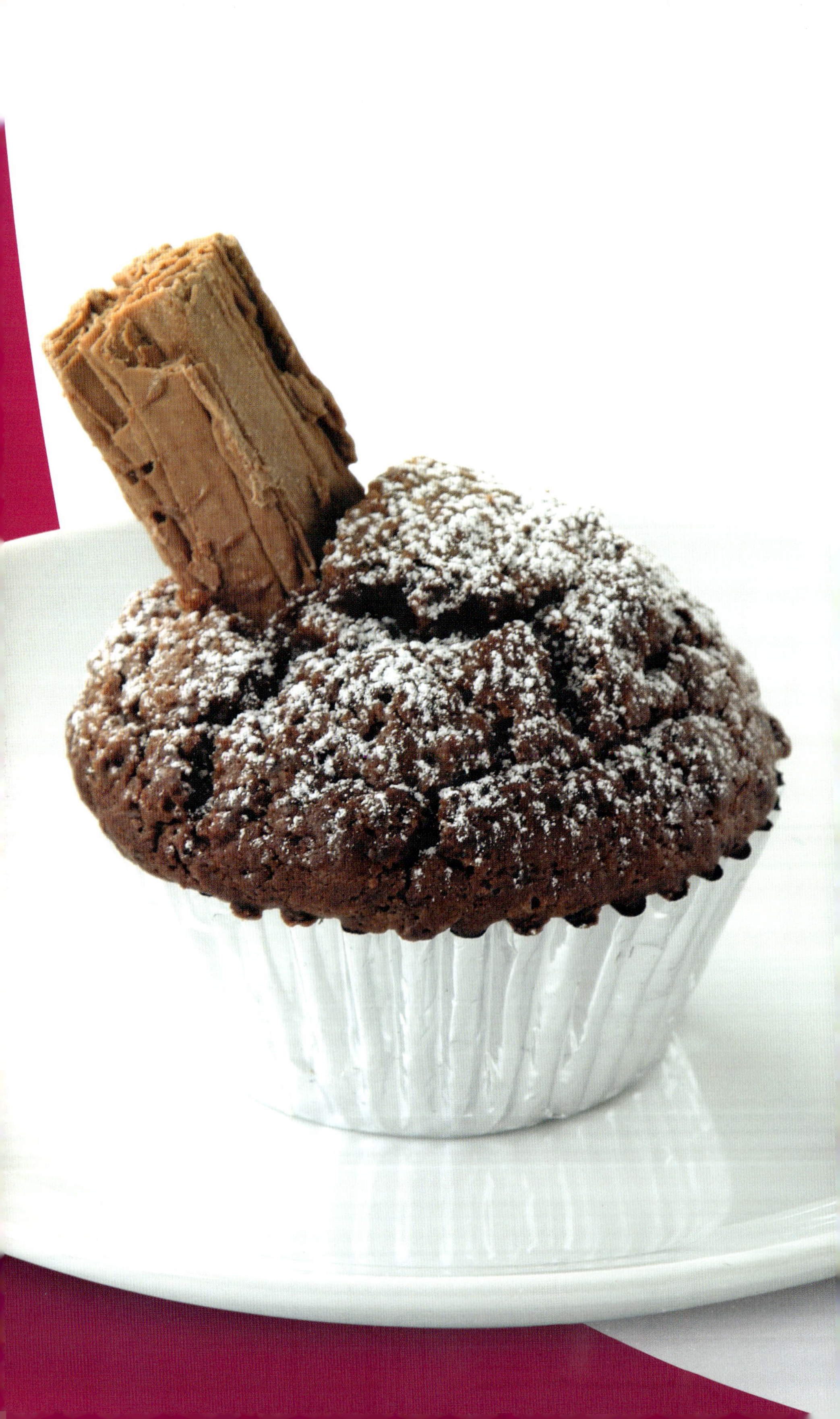

BAKING

These simple recipes are **fun** to make and really **yummy** — great for parties and morning tea and picnics and afternoon tea and …

Chocolate Brownie Muffin (pages 102 and 103)

BANANA CHOCOLATE CHIP MUFFINS

Makes 12 large muffins

The secret to great-looking muffins is not to overmix when combining the liquid and dry ingredients. The mixture often appears lumpy — this is how it should look.

- 2½ cups Champion standard grade flour
- ¾ cup brown sugar
- 4 teaspoons Edmonds baking powder
- ½ teaspoon Edmonds baking soda
- 1 teaspoon cinnamon
- ¾ cup chocolate chips
- 1 cup milk
- 2 eggs
- 125 g butter, melted
- 1 teaspoon vanilla essence
- ¾ cup mashed banana (about 2 medium bananas)

1 Grease 12 deep muffin tins (including rims) or line with paper cases then grease. Preheat the oven to 200°C.

2 Mix the flour, brown sugar, baking powder, baking soda and cinnamon together in a large bowl. Stir in the chocolate chips.

3 In another bowl, whisk together the milk, eggs, butter and essence.

4 Lightly mix the egg mixture and banana into the dry ingredients until just combined. Do not overmix.

5 Divide the mixture between the prepared tins. Bake for 20 minutes or until well risen and a light gold colour.

6 Stand the muffins for 5 minutes before removing them from the tins.

> Spread cooled muffins with Cream Cheese Icing (page 130). Arrange small, dried banana chips on top of the muffins.

BERRY MUFFINS

Makes 12 large muffins

Delicious served for breakfast, lunch or as a snack. You can use any kind of fresh or frozen berries. These muffins freeze well.

2½ cups Champion standard grade flour
4 teaspoons Edmonds baking powder
1 cup sugar
1 teaspoon cinnamon
1½ cups fresh or frozen berries (see Cook's Tip), e.g. blueberries, quartered strawberries, raspberries or any combination of these
1¼ cups milk
¼ cup Amco canola oil
2 eggs
icing sugar to dust

1. Grease 12 deep muffin tins and rims or line tins with paper cases, then grease. Preheat the oven to 200°C.

2. Mix the flour, baking powder, sugar and cinnamon together in a large bowl. Add the berries and toss lightly to coat with flour.

3. In another bowl, whisk together the milk, oil and eggs. Pour the liquid ingredients over the dry ingredients. Mix lightly until just combined — do not overmix.

4 Divide the mixture between the prepared tins. Bake for 20–25 minutes until well risen.

5 Let the muffins stand for 5 minutes before removing them from the tins. If you like, dust with icing sugar just before serving.

Do not thaw frozen berries before using.

CHOCOLATE BROWNIE MUFFINS

Makes 12 large muffins

These delicious muffins are really like mini cakes and are great for a special occasion. The simple but clever serving ideas below transform them into a stunning dessert or even individual birthday cakes that friends can take home with them.

125 g dark chocolate (Energy chocolate is ideal), broken into pieces
125 g butter, chopped
2½ cups Champion standard grade flour
4 teaspoons Edmonds baking powder
⅓ cup cocoa
1¼ cups sugar
½ cup roughly chopped walnuts, optional
1¼ cups milk
2 eggs
1 teaspoon vanilla essence

1 Place the chocolate and butter in a heatproof (glass or stainless) bowl or in the top of a double boiler. Sit over a pan of simmering (just boiling) water.

2 Stir constantly until the mixture is smooth. Remove from the heat.

3 Preheat the oven to 200°C. Grease 12 deep muffin tins (including rims) or line with paper cases then grease.

4 Sift the flour, baking powder and cocoa into a large bowl. Stir in the sugar and walnuts.

5 In another bowl whisk together the milk, eggs and essence.

6 Pour the chocolate mixture and milk over the dry ingredients. Mix lightly until the ingredients are just combined. Do not overmix.

7 Divide the mixture between the prepared tins. Bake for 20 minutes. Stand the muffins for 5 minutes before removing them from the tins.

Serving Suggestions
- Serve at room temperature, dusted with icing sugar.
- For delicious individual desserts, scoop out a little of the middle of each muffin. Fill each hole with a small scoop of ice-cream. Place on a serving plate.
- Give friends a lovely treat to take home at the end of a birthday party — use a sharp knife to remove a small tunnel of muffin. Place a mini Flake bar or wafer biscuit in the hole. Dust with icing sugar. (See the photograph on page 96.)
- Have fun using coloured icing, sprinkles and silver balls (called cachous) to decorate muffins. (See the photograph on the front cover of this book.)

SCONES

Makes 12

Once you have mastered scone making you are well on your way to being a fabulous cook! One of the secrets to great scones is to mix the dough quickly without overworking it.

3 cups Champion standard grade flour
6 teaspoons Edmonds baking powder
¼ teaspoon salt
75 g butter, chopped
1–1½ cups milk
extra milk to brush

1 Preheat the oven to 220°C. Lightly dust an oven tray with flour or line with baking paper.

2 Sift the flour, baking powder and salt into a large bowl. Cut the butter into the flour until it resembles fine breadcrumbs. (You can use a food processor to do this.)

3 Add the milk and mix quickly to a soft dough with a knife.

4 Knead a few times, then transfer the dough to the oven tray. Press the dough into a 14 cm x 18 cm rectangle (about 3 cm thick).

5 Cut into 12 even-sized pieces. Place 2 cm apart on the baking tray.

6 Brush the tops with milk. Bake for 10 minutes until golden.

Cheese Scones: Add ¾ cup grated cheddar cheese to flour after cutting in the butter.

Sultana Scones: Add ¾ cup sultanas to the flour after cutting in the butter.

> Serve a Devonshire Tea — this is guaranteed to be a favourite with parents and grandparents! Serve warm plain Scones (not cheese or sultana) with whipped cream and your favourite jam. Accompany with a cup of freshly brewed tea or coffee.

BANANA BREAD

This moist, cake-like bread is yummy sliced and spread with butter.

125 g butter, chopped
¾ cup brown sugar
¼ cup golden syrup
2 cups Champion standard grade flour
2 teaspoons Edmonds baking powder
1 teaspoon ground ginger
1 teaspoon cinnamon
2 eggs, lightly beaten
1 cup mashed ripe banana (2 large bananas)
½ cup chopped walnuts, optional

1 Grease a 23 cm x 13 cm loaf tin. Line the base with baking paper. Preheat the oven to 180°C.

2 Place the butter, brown sugar and golden syrup in a saucepan. Stir over a low heat until the butter has melted. Cool for 5–10 minutes.

3 Sift the flour, baking powder, ginger and cinnamon into a bowl. Make a well in the centre.

4 Add the cooled butter mixture, eggs, banana and walnuts. Mix lightly until smooth.

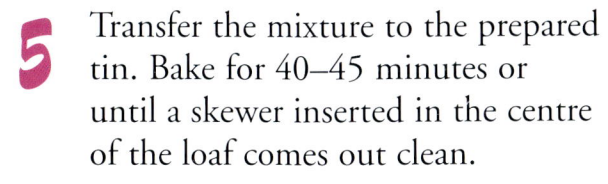

5 Transfer the mixture to the prepared tin. Bake for 40–45 minutes or until a skewer inserted in the centre of the loaf comes out clean.

6 Stand for 5 minutes before turning onto a wire rack. Cool. Cut into slices and serve with butter.

AFGHANS

Makes 22

A crunchy, chocolatey New Zealand classic.

200 g butter, softened
½ cup sugar
1 ¼ cups Champion standard grade flour
¼ cup cocoa
2 cups cornflakes
Chocolate Icing (page 130)
walnuts, optional

1 Grease 2 oven trays. Preheat the oven to 180°C. Beat the butter and sugar until light and creamy.

2 Sift the flour and cocoa. Stir into the butter mixture.

3 Fold in the cornflakes.

4 Spoon mounds of the mixture onto the oven trays, gently pressing the mixture together.

5 Bake for 15 minutes or until set. Transfer to a wire rack to cool.

6 When cold, ice with Chocolate Icing and decorate with a walnut.

The Afghan mixture can be made into an Afghan Slice. Grease a 20 cm x 30 cm sponge roll tin. Press the mixture into the tin. Bake at 180°C for 25 minutes. Remove from the oven and place on a wire rack to cool. When cold, spread with Chocolate Icing. Once the icing is set, cut into slices.

CHOCOLATE CHUNK COOKIES

Makes 27 cookies

Popular with everyone! These Chocolate Chunk Cookies are a great after-school snack or lunchbox filler.

    125 g butter, softened
    1 cup brown sugar (pack sugar firmly into the measuring cup)
    1 egg
    1 teaspoon vanilla essence
    1½ cups Champion standard grade flour
    ½ teaspoon Edmonds baking powder
    ½ cup (100 g) chopped dark chocolate (or chocolate chips)

1 Grease an oven try. Preheat the oven to 180°C.

2 Using an electric beater, beat together butter and sugar until creamy. Add the egg and essence. Beat well.

3 Sift the flour and baking powder into a bowl.

4 Stir the flour and chocolate into the butter mixture. Mix well.

5 Drop tablespoonsful of the mixture onto oven trays, allowing 3–4 cm between biscuits for spreading. (You may need to use a knife to help the mixture out of the measuring spoon.)

6 Bake for 18–20 minutes until golden. Stand for 2–3 minutes before transferring to a wire rack to cool.

> Half-and-Half Biscuits — use ¼ cup (50 g) each of chopped white chocolate and chopped dark chocolate.

HOKEY POKEY BISCUITS

Makes 22

Famous in New Zealand — the ice-cream as well as the biscuits!

125 g butter
½ cup caster sugar
1 tablespoon golden syrup
1 tablespoon milk
1½ cups Champion standard grade flour
1 teaspoon Edmonds baking soda

1 Preheat the oven to 180°C. Grease an oven tray. Place the butter, sugar, golden syrup and milk in a saucepan. Stir over a low heat until the butter has melted. Increase the heat and continue stirring until the mixture almost bubbles.

2 Remove the saucepan from the heat and allow mixture to cool.

3 Sift the flour and baking soda into a bowl. Stir the flour into the butter mixture. Mix well.

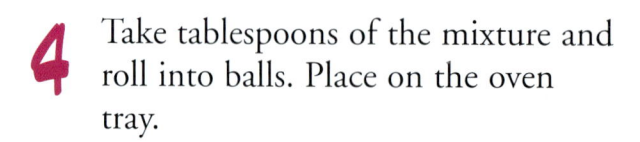

4 Take tablespoons of the mixture and roll into balls. Place on the oven tray.

5 Flatten the biscuits slightly with a floured fork. Bake for 15–20 minutes or until golden. Transfer to a wire rack to cool.

Homemade biscuits make a great gift for friends and family that will be much appreciated. Place the biscuits, in a stack, in small cellophane bags (available from homeware stores), pushing out any air from the package so they stay fresh. Allow enough cellophane at the top of the bags to gather together. Firmly tie with a length of ribbon, string or try using a narrow strip of flax.

MELTING MOMENTS

Makes 16

Soft, melting and yummy. Try sandwiching them together with Passionfruit Icing — add 1 tablespoon of passionfruit pulp before the boiling water when you make the Vanilla Icing.

200 g butter, softened
¾ cup icing sugar
1 cup Champion standard grade flour
1 cup Edmonds Fielder's cornflour
½ teaspoon Edmonds baking powder

Vanilla Icing
1 cup icing sugar
¼ teaspoon vanilla essence
1 teaspoon butter
a little boiling water to mix

1. Grease 2 oven trays. Preheat the oven to 180°C.

2. Beat the butter and icing sugar until light and creamy.

3. Sift the flour, cornflour and baking powder into a bowl. Add to the creamed mixture. Mix well.

4 Roll the dough into small balls (the size of large marbles) and place on oven trays.

5 Flatten slightly with a floured fork. Bake for 20 minutes. Transfer to wire racks. When cold, sandwich 2 biscuits together with Vanilla Icing.

6 To make the icing, place the icing sugar, essence and butter in a bowl. Add enough water to mix to a spreadable consistency.

CUP CAKES

Decorating Cup Cakes is a lot of fun. You can match the icing colours to the colour of the paper patty cases. Make Cup Cakes on the day they are to be served.

125 g butter, softened
1 teaspoon vanilla essence
¾ cup caster sugar
2 eggs
1½ cups Champion standard grade flour
1½ teaspoons Edmonds baking powder
½ cup milk
Vanilla Icing (page 114)

1 Place 12 large paper patty cases in deep muffin tins. Preheat the oven to 180°C.

2 Beat together the butter, essence and sugar until light and creamy. Add the eggs one at a time, beating well after each addition.

3 Sift the flour and baking powder into a bowl. Fold the flour into the butter mixture. Stir in the milk.

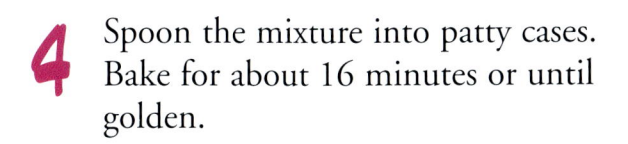

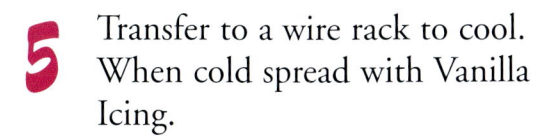

4 Spoon the mixture into patty cases. Bake for about 16 minutes or until golden.

5 Transfer to a wire rack to cool. When cold spread with Vanilla Icing.

> Decorate your Cup Cakes with silver cachous (little silver balls), sprinkles of different colours and shapes, or even candles for Birthday Cup Cakes! Decorations are available from supermarkets and kitchenware stores.

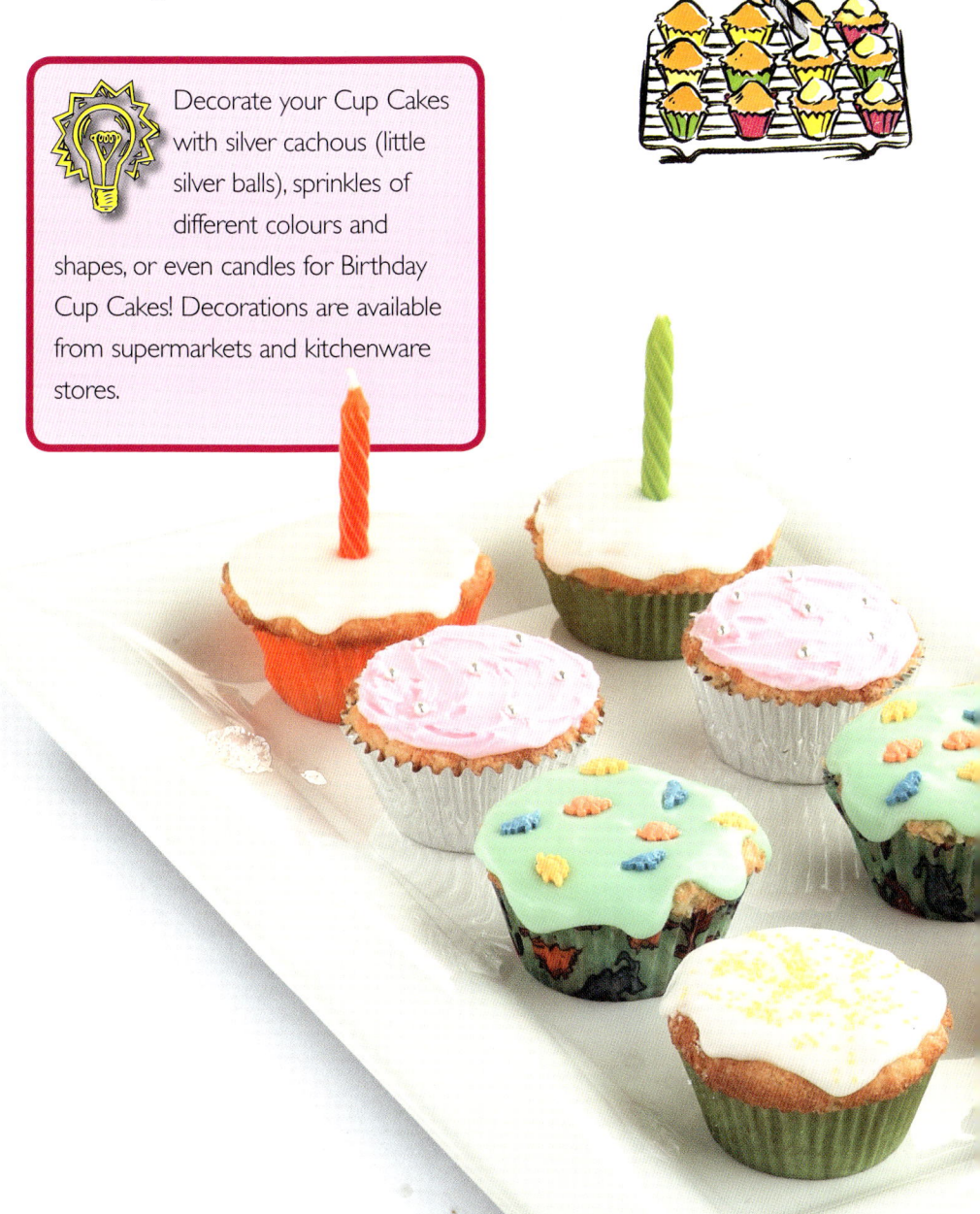

FRUIT-BIX BARS

This tasty fruit and Weet-Bix slice is breakfast-in-a-bar! If you're in a hurry or need an energy boost after early morning sports practice Fruit-bix Bars are perfect. They are also a great lunchbox filler.

100 g butter, chopped
½ cup sugar
½ cup liquid honey
1 cup Champion standard grade flour
1 teaspoon Edmonds baking powder
1 cup coconut
1 cup dried fruit, e.g. sultanas, raisins, currants, chopped dried apricots
½ cup rolled oats
½ cup sunflower seeds
1 egg, lightly beaten
½ cup mashed banana (about 1 large banana)
5 Weet-Bix, crushed (see Cook's Tip)

1 Grease a 20 cm x 30 cm shallow baking tin. Line the base with baking paper. Preheat the oven to 180°C.

2 Place the butter, sugar and honey in a small saucepan. Stir over a low heat until the butter melts. Remove from the heat.

3 Combine the flour, baking powder, coconut, dried fruit, rolled oats and sunflower seeds in a large bowl.

4 Pour the butter mixture and egg over the dry ingredients. Mix well.

5 Add the banana and Weet-Bix. Mix well. Spread the mixture evenly over the base of the tin.

6 Bake for 20–25 minutes, until golden. Cool in the tin. When cold, cut into bars.

To crush Weet-Bix, scrunch them with clean hands over a bowl. Do not flake too finely.

Nutty Crunch Slice

Crammed full of seeds and nuts, this delicious slice needs to be kept in the refrigerator. You will need a food processor to make this recipe.

1 cup sesame seeds
1 cup pumpkin seeds
1 cup coconut
1 cup chopped Brazil nuts
250 g packet Gingernut biscuits
½ cup chopped dried apricots
1 teaspoon ground ginger
125 g butter, chopped
½ cup sweetened condensed milk

1 Lightly grease a 20 cm x 30 cm shallow baking tin. Place the sesame seeds, pumpkin seeds, coconut and Brazil nuts in a non-stick frying pan.

2 Stir constantly over a low-medium heat for 6–8 minutes until the mixture starts to pop and the coconut turns a light golden colour. Transfer to a bowl.

3 Place the Gingernuts in a food processor and process until they are fine crumbs.

4 Stir the crumbs, apricots and ginger into the toasted mixture.

5 Place the butter and condensed milk in a small saucepan. Stir over a low heat until the butter has melted. Pour over the dry ingredients and mix well.

6 Press the mixture over the base of the tin. Cover and refrigerate for 1 hour before cutting into shapes of your choice. Cover and store in the refrigerator.

THE BEST CHOCOLATE BROWNIES

Perfect for a celebration, to take on a picnic, or eat them with ice-cream for dessert.

    175 g butter, chopped
    250 g dark chocolate (Energy or cooking chocolate), broken into pieces
    1½ cups Champion standard grade flour
    1 cup sugar
    2 teaspoons vanilla essence
    3 eggs, beaten
    1 cup chopped walnuts, optional
    icing sugar to dust

1 Grease a 20 cm square baking tin. Line the base with baking paper. Preheat the oven to 180°C.

2 Place the butter and chocolate in a medium saucepan. Stir constantly over a very low heat until melted. Remove from the heat.

3 Stir in the flour, sugar, essence, eggs and walnuts. Pour the mixture into the tin.

4 Bake for 40 minutes — the surface should be slightly cracked.

5 Leave in the tin for 10 minutes before turning out onto a wire rack to cool. Cut into squares. Just before serving, dust with icing sugar.

> Blonde Brownies — replace the dark chocolate with white chocolate.

BANANA CAKE

Deliciously moist, this Banana Cake will vanish in a flash!

125 g butter, softened
¾ cup sugar
2 eggs
1½ cups mashed ripe banana (about 4 medium bananas)
1 teaspoon Edmonds baking soda
2 tablespoons warm milk (see Cook's Tip)
2 cups Champion standard grade flour
1 teaspoon Edmonds baking powder
Lemon Icing (page 131)
lemon zest to garnish, optional

1 Grease a 20-cm round cake tin. Line the base with baking paper. Preheat the oven to 180°C.

2 Using an electric mixer, beat the butter and sugar until light and creamy. Add the eggs one at a time, beating well after each addition.

3 Add the mashed banana and mix thoroughly. Stir the baking soda into the warm milk and add to the creamed mixture.

4 Sift the flour and baking powder. Fold into the banana mixture.

5 Transfer to the cake tin. Bake for 50 minutes or until a skewer pushed into the centre of the cake comes out clean. Leave the cake in the tin for 10 minutes before turning it out onto a wire rack to cool.

6 When cold, ice with Lemon Icing. Garnish with lemon zest, if you like. (Lemon zest is the outer rind, not the white pith.)

> To warm milk, place in a small microwave-proof container. Heat on high power for 10 seconds.

CARROT CAKE

As good as any café cake!

¾ cup Amco canola oil
1 cup firmly packed brown sugar
3 eggs
2 cups Champion standard grade flour
2 teaspoons Edmonds baking powder
½ teaspoon Edmonds baking soda
1 teaspoon cinnamon
3 cups firmly packed grated carrot (about 3 large carrots)
½ cup chopped walnuts
Cream Cheese Icing (page 130)
chopped walnuts, pumpkin seeds and dried pineapple or rockmelon to garnish, optional

1 Grease a 20 cm round cake tin. Line the base with baking paper. Preheat the oven to 180°C.

2 Beat the oil, sugar and eggs with an electric mixer for 5 minutes until thick.

3 Sift the flour, baking powder, baking soda and cinnamon.

4 Fold the carrot and walnuts into the egg mixture. Lastly, fold in the dry ingredients.

5 Place the mixture in the cake tin. Bake for 1 hour or until a skewer pushed into the centre of the cake comes out clean. Stand the cake in the tin for 10 minutes before turning it out onto a wire rack to cool.

6 When cold, ice with Cream Cheese Icing. If you like, sprinkle with walnuts, pumpkin seeds and dried pineapple or rockmelon.

CHOCOLATE CAKE

Who doesn't love chocolate cake? The perfect birthday cake.

125 g butter, chopped
1 cup milk
½ teaspoon Edmonds baking soda
2 cups Champion standard grade flour
2 teaspoons Edmonds baking powder
¼ cup cocoa
¾ cup sugar
1 teaspoon vanilla essence
2 eggs
Chocolate Icing (page 130)

1 Preheat the oven to 180°C. Grease a 20-cm diameter tin. Line the base with baking paper.

2 Place the butter and milk in a saucepan. Stir over a low heat until the butter is melted. Remove from the heat. Stir in the baking soda. Leave to cool for 10 minutes.

3 Sift the flour, baking powder and cocoa into a large bowl. Stir in sugar.

4 Whisk the essence and eggs into the cooled butter mixture. Pour the butter mixture over the flour. Mix lightly until the ingredients are combined.

5 Transfer the mixture to the tin. Bake for 45 minutes. Leave the cake in the tin for 5 minutes, then turn onto a wire rack to cool.

6 When the cake is cold, spread with Chocolate Icing.

ICINGS

Chocolate Icing
2 cups icing sugar
2 tablespoons cocoa
¼ teaspoon butter
¼ teaspoon vanilla essence
about 2 tablespoons boiling water

1 Sift the icing sugar and cocoa into a bowl.

2 Add the butter and vanilla essence.

3 Add enough boiling water to mix to a spreadable consistency.

Cream Cheese Icing
1 cup icing sugar
150 g spreadable cream cheese
1 teaspoon lemon juice

1 Sift the icing sugar into a bowl.

2 Add the cream cheese and lemon juice.

3 Beat until combined. (This can be done with an electric mixer.)

Vanilla Icing

1 cup icing sugar
¼ teaspoon vanilla essence
1 teaspoon butter
a little boiling water to mix

1 Place the icing sugar, essence and butter in a bowl.

2 Add enough boiling water to mix to a spreadable consistency.

Lemon Icing

1 cup icing sugar
1 teaspoon lemon juice
1 teaspoon butter
a little boiling water to mix

1 Place the icing sugar, lemon juice and butter in a bowl.

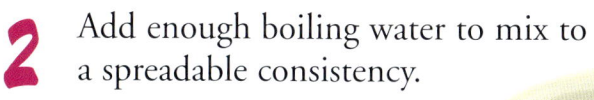

2 Add enough boiling water to mix to a spreadable consistency.

MENU IDEAS

SLEEPOVER

Planning to have a few friends for a sleepover? Falafel in Pita Bread will go down a treat and these ideas won't break the bank either! You will need to cook the falafels just before serving, but they can be prepared ahead of time and refrigerated. The Hummus, Tabbouleh and Chocolate Brownies can be made well in advance.

Falafel in Pita Bread (page 42)
Hummus (page 18)
Tabbouleh (page 38)
The Best Chocolate Brownies (page 122)

DVD EVENING

While you're watching a movie, serve Hummus and Guacamole with toasted Turkish bread, pita bread or crackers. Prepare Pizza Dough before your friends arrive. Once the dough has been kneaded, place in the refrigerator in a greased, covered bowl. It will rise slowly, over a period of several hours. Prepare a selection of topping ingredients in advance and get your friends to create their own pizza. Then finish off with a slice of yummy Carrot Cake.

Hummus (page 18)
Guacamole (page 19)
Pizza (page 54)
Carrot Cake (page 126)

SPECIAL DINNER

Your guests will be very impressed with the following three-course dinner! The Meringue Nests can be made well in advance. Make the Pesto and

Bruschetta in advance too, then assemble just before serving. Serve the Roast Chicken with roast vegetables and a seasonal green vegetable. Serve with a seasonal green vegetable such as beans, broccoli or Brussels sprouts.

    Basil Pesto and Tomato Bruschetta (pages 20 and 22)
    Roast Chicken with Moroccan Couscous Stuffing (page 78)
    Meringue Nests (page 90)

FRIENDS FOR WEEKEND BRUNCH

Brunch on a lazy weekend morning is a great opportunity to gather together friends or family. Allow yourself enough time to make the muffins so they are still warm when served. The Marshmallow Yoghurt Cream can be made the night before too. Prepare the fresh fruit several hours in advance. The French Toast will need to be cooked just before serving. If you can't get fresh croissants on the day, they can be purchased in advance from most supermarkets — check the use-by date.

    Fruit Salad with Marshmallow Yoghurt Cream (page 82)
    Berry Muffins (page 100)
    French Toast (page 14)
    Ham and Cheese Croissants: slice croissants horizontally. Insert a slice of gruyere cheese and a slice of ham. Warm in a 180°C oven for 10 minutes, if you like.

PACK A PICNIC

Take time out from your busy life and arrange to meet friends or family for a picnic. During summer months it is important to pack food in a chilled container to prevent the risk of food poisoning — bacteria thrive in warm conditions. Make the Ham Frittata in advance and allow to cool to room temperature, then cut into wedges and wrap in foil.

    Ham Frittata (page 44)
    Green Salad: make a salad with lettuce, sliced cucumber and tomato wedges. Place in a sealed container. Pack an avocado and slice into salad just before serving. Take salad dressing of your choice in a separate container and toss through salad just before serving.
    Fresh Crusty Bread
    Melting Moments (page 114)

INDEX

Afghans 108–9
apples: Little Apple Pies 88–9
avocados
    Guacamole 19
    Stuffed Baked Potatoes 46–7
    Tuna Salad 36–7

bacon
    Caesar Salad 34–5
    French Toast 14–5
    Pasta alla Carbonara 48–9
    Pasta with Pesto, Bacon and Peas 50–1
    Stuffed Baked Potatoes 46–7
bananas
    Banana Bread 106–7
    Banana Cake 124–5
    Banana Chocolate Chip Muffins 98–9
    Fruit-bix Bars 118–9
    Pancakes 12–3
Basil Pesto 20
Basil Pesto and Tomato Topping 22
beans, dried
    Nachos 62–3
    Stuffed Baked Potatoes 46–7
beef
    Hamburgers 60–1
    Lasagne 66–7
    Nachos 62–3
    Spaghetti and Meatballs 64–5
    Thai-style Stir-fried Beef with Peanuts 74–5
    Wiener Schnitzel 68–9
Berry Muffins 100–1
Best Chocolate Brownies 122–3
biscuits and slices
    Afghans 108–9
    Best Chocolate Brownies 122–3
    Chocolate Chunk Cookies 110–1
    Fruit-bix Bars 118–9
    Hokey Pokey Biscuits 112–3
    Melting Moments 114–5
    Nutty Crunch Slice 120–1
blueberries: Berry Muffins 100–1
Bruschetta 22–3

Caesar Salad 34–5
cakes
    Banana Cake 124–5
    Carrot Cake 126–7
    Chocolate Cake 128–9
    Cup Cakes 116–7
Caramel Sauce 94
cheese
    Caesar Salad 34–5
    Cheese and Salsa Quesadillas 26–7
    Cheese Scones 105
    Ham and Cheese Croissants 133
    Lasagne 66–7
    Macaroni Cheese 52–3
    Nachos 62–3
    Omelette 40–1
    Pasta alla Carbonara 48–9
    Pizza Toppings 56
    Sausages with Mash and Cheese 76–7
    Stuffed Baked Potatoes 46–7
    Walnut Pesto, Pear and Parmesan Topping 23
chicken
    Cheese and Salsa Quesadillas 26–7
    Chicken and Pesto Pizza 56
    Chicken Caesar Salad 35
    Chicken Kebabs with Quick Peanut Sauce 58–9
    Chicken with Beans and Hokkien Noodles 72–3
    Chicken Wraps 24–5
    Corn and Chicken Soup 30–1
    Roast Chicken with Moroccan Couscous Stuffing 78–9
chickpeas
    Falafel in Pita Bread with Garlic Sauce 42–3
    Hummus 18
chocolate
    Afghans 108–9
    Banana Chocolate Chip Muffins 98–9
    Best Chocolate Brownies 122–3
    Chocolate Almond and Apricot Clusters 85
    Chocolate Brownie Muffins 102–3
    Chocolate Cake 128–9
    Chocolate Chunk Cookies 110–1
    Chocolate Icing 130

Chocolate Sauce 95
Chocolate-dipped Treats 84–5
Jewelled Chocolate Discs 85
Semifreddo 92–3
coconut
   Fruit-bix Bars 118–9
   Nutty Crunch Slice 120–1
   Semifreddo 92–3
   Toasted Muesli 10–1
Corn and Chicken Soup 30–1
couscous: Roast Chicken with Moroccan Couscous Stuffing 78–9
Cream Cheese Icing 130
Cup Cakes 116–7

eggs
   French Toast 14–5
   Ham Frittata 44–5
   Omelette 40–1
   Pasta alla Carbonara 48–9

Falafel in Pita Bread with Garlic Sauce 42–3
French Toast 14–5
frittata, ham 44–5
Fruit and Yoghurt Smoothie 17
Fruit-bix Bars 118–9
fruit, dried
   Chocolate Almond and Apricot Clusters 85
   Fruit-bix Bars 118–9
   Jewelled Chocolate Discs 85
   Toasted Muesli 10–1
Fruit Salad 82–3
Fudge Pudding 86–7

Garlic Sauce 43
gingernut biscuits: Nutty Crunch Slice 120–1
Greek Pizza 56
Guacamole 19

ham
   Ham and Cheese Croissants 133
   Ham Frittata 44–5
   Hawaiian Pizza 56
Hamburgers 60–1
Hawaiian Pizza 56
Hokey Pokey Biscuits 112–3
Hummus 18

ice-cream
   Ice-cream Sauces 94–5
   Semifreddo 92–3

icing
   Chocolate Icing 130
   Cream Cheese Icing 130
   Lemon Icing 131
   Passionfruit Icing 114
   Vanilla Icing 114, 131

Jewelled Chocolate Discs 85

kebabs, chicken, with quick peanut sauce 58–9

Lasagne 66–7
Lemon Icing 131
Little Apple Pies 88–9

Macaroni Cheese 52–3
Marshmallow Yoghurt Cream 82–3
Mashed Potatoes 69
Melting Moments 114–5
Meringue Nests 90–1
mince – see beef
muesli, toasted 10–1
muffins
   Banana Chocolate Chip Muffins 98–9
   Berry Muffins 100–1
   Chocolate Brownie Muffins 102–3
mushrooms
   Chicken Kebabs with Quick Peanut Sauce 58–9
   Mushroom and Salami Pizza 56

Nachos 62–3
noodles: Chicken with Beans and Hokkien Noodles 72–73
nuts and seeds
   Chocolate Almond and Apricot Clusters 85
   Fruit-bix Bars 118–9
   Jewelled Chocolate Discs 85
   Nutty Crunch Slice 120–1
   Toasted Muesli 10–1

Omelette 40–1

Pancakes 12–3
parmesan cheese – see cheese
passionfruit
   Passionfruit Crème Fraîche 83
   Passionfruit Icing 114
   Semifreddo 92–3
pasta
   Macaroni Cheese 52–3
   Pasta alla Carbonara 48–9

Pasta with Pesto, Bacon and Peas 50–1
Spaghetti and Meatballs 64–5
peanuts
    Quick Peanut Sauce 59
    Thai-style Stir-fried Beef with Peanuts 74–5
pears: Walnut Pesto, Pear and Parmesan Topping 23
peas: Pasta with Pesto, Bacon and Peas 50–1
peppers
    Chicken Kebabs with Quick Peanut Sauce 58–9
    Mushroom and Salami Pizza 56
    Thai-style Sweet and Sour Pork Stir-fry 70–1
pesto
    Basil Pesto 20
    Chicken and Pesto Pizza 56
    Pasta with Pesto, Bacon and Peas 50–1
    Walnut and Parsley Pesto 20
pies, little apple 88–9
pineapple
    Chicken Kebabs with Quick Peanut Sauce 58–9
    Hawaiian Pizza 56
    Thai-style Sweet and Sour Pork Stir-fry 70–1
pita bread, falafel in 42–3
Pizza Base 54–5
Pizza Toppings 56
pork: Thai-style Sweet and Sour Pork Stir-fry 70–1
potatoes
    Ham Frittata 44–5
    Mashed Potatoes 69
    Pumpkin Soup 28–9
    Sausages with Mash and Cheese 76–7
    Stuffed Baked Potatoes 46–7
Pumpkin Soup 28–9

quesadillas, cheese and salsa 26–7
Quick Peanut Sauce 59

raspberries
    Berry Muffins 100–1
    Semifreddo 92–3
Roast Chicken with Moroccan Couscous Stuffing 78–9

salads
    Caesar Salad 34–5
    Green Salad 133
    Tuna Salad 36–7
salami: Mushroom and Salami Pizza 56
sauces
    Caramel Sauce 94
    Chocolate Sauce 95
    Garlic Sauce 43

Quick Peanut Sauce 59
Sausages with Mash and Cheese 76–7
Scones 104–5
seeds – *see* nuts and seeds
Semifreddo 92–3
slices – *see* biscuits and slices
Slushies 16
smoothie, fruit and yoghurt 17
soups
    Corn and Chicken Soup 30–1
    Pumpkin Soup 28–9
Spaghetti and Meatballs 64–5
strawberries
    Berry Muffins 100–1
    Chocolate-dipped Treats 84–5
Stuffed Baked Potatoes 46–7
Sultana Scones 105

Tabbouleh 38–9
Thai-style Stir-fried Beef with Peanuts 74–5
Thai-style Sweet and Sour Pork Stir-fry 70–1
Toasted Muesli 10–1
tomatoes
    Basil Pesto and Tomato Topping 22
    Nachos 62–3
    Pasta with Pesto, Bacon and Peas 50–1
    Pizza Toppings 56
    Tabbouleh 38–9
    Thai-style Sweet and Sour Pork Stir-fry 70–1
    Tuna Salad 36–7
tuna
    Stuffed Baked Potatoes 46–7
    Tuna Salad 36–7

Vanilla Icing 114, 131

walnuts
    Carrot Cake 126–7
    Pasta with Pesto, Bacon and Peas 50–1
    Walnut and Parsley Pesto 20
    Walnut Pesto, Pear and Parmesan Topping 23
Weet-Bix: Fruit-bix Bars 118–9
Wiener Schnitzel 68–9
wraps, chicken 24–5

yoghurt
    Fruit and Yoghurt Smoothie 17
    Garlic Sauce 43
    Marshmallow Yoghurt Cream 82–3